101 Business Tax Tips

2023/24

By

Sarah Bradford

Publisher Details
This guide is published by Tax Insider Ltd, 3 Sanderson Close, Great Sankey, Warrington WA5 3LN.

'101 Business Tax Tips' (formerly 101 Business Tax Secrets Revealed and 101 Tax Tips for Entrepreneurs) first published in September 2012, second edition April 2013, third edition April 2014, fourth edition September 2015, fifth edition May 2016, sixth edition April 2019, seventh edition September 2020, eighth edition July 2021, ninth edition May 2022, tenth edition May 2023.

ISBN 978-1-7394249-0-9

Contents

About This Guide

All businesses, large or small, like to save tax and there are many simple steps that a business can take to achieve this aim.

This guide contains 101 tax savings tips aimed at entrepreneurs. The tips follow the lifecycle of a business meaning that there is something for everyone, regardless of whether you are thinking of starting a business, a new start-up or an established business. Many of the tips apply equally to sole traders, partnerships and companies, whereas some are specific to a particular type of business.

However, it should be noted that tips in this guide are for illustration purposes only and are intended to demonstrate where tax savings can be made. The savings that can be made will depend on the precise circumstances and the examples are a guide only. Professional advice should always be sought.

Chapter 1.
Business Structure

1. Choose The Right Structure For Your Business

2. Choose Which Taxes You Pay

3. Take Advantage Of The Veil Of Incorporation

4. Save Incorporation Costs

5. Create Different Categories Of Shares In A Limited Company

6. Keep Administration Costs Low

7. Keep All Business Profits For Yourself

8. Maximise The Skill Base

9. Agree The Split Of Partnership Profits And Losses

10. Consider Purchasing An Existing Business

11. Run A Franchise

1.   Choose The Right Structure For Your Business

There are various ways in which businesses can be structured, and it is important that the structure that is chosen is the right one for the business.

There are four main options:

- sole trader;
- partnership;
- limited liability partnership; and
- limited company.

The choice of business vehicle affects the type of taxes you pay, your liability for business debts and the legal and administrative requirements imposed on the business. It will also affect the way in which business decisions are made and the sources of finance available to the business.

In deciding on the right structure for the business, it is necessary to take account of all relevant factors and also your attitude to risk.

For example, a sole trader is the simplest set-up and the proprietor gets to keep all of the profits. However, he or she is also liable for all of the business debts. The sole trader is taxed on his or her total income after deducting his or her personal allowances – the profits of the business are not taxed separately but form part of the sole trader's taxable income, together with income from other sources, such as any employment or investment income. A sole trader must also pay Class 2 and Class 4 National Insurance contributions (NICs) if profits exceed the relevant trigger thresholds.

A limited company is more complicated to set up and administer, but the shareholders' liability is limited to the amount of capital that they own – a major plus. The company is taxed in its own right, and any profits that are extracted from the company will be taxed on the recipients. The tax position of the company is separate from that of the individual shareholders. The company must file annual accounts and an annual confirmation statement at Companies House. Being a director of a limited company also confers certain statutory duties.

Choose The Right Structure For Your Business

Bill wants to set up his own business. He has some money to invest but does not want to risk losing his family home if the business fails.

He is also keen to present a professional image to potential customers to help him win new business.

Having considered all the factors, Bill decides that a limited company is the right vehicle for his business. Limited liability is very important to him and he is prepared to undertake the additional administrative burden associated with a limited company in return for this.

2.   Choose Which Taxes You Pay

The choice of business vehicle will also determine which taxes are paid by your business. Sole traders and partnerships pay income tax on their profits and Class 2 and Class 4 NICs whereas a limited company pays corporation tax. However, there may also be income tax to pay on profits extracted from a limited company and where those profits are extracted in the form of a salary or bonus, Class 1 NICs.

The profits from a sole trader's business and a partner's share of partnership profits are taken into account in working out his or her overall income tax liability, together with income from other sources, such as any employment income, taxable interest and dividend income. Personal allowances are available to reduce the amount on which tax is charged. To the extent that business profits exceed the proprietor's personal allowance, they are taxed at 20%, 40% or 45% for taxpayers in the UK excluding Scotland (the Scottish rates of income tax apply to Scottish taxpayers).

By contrast, the taxable profits of a company are taxed at the corporation tax rate, which for the financial year 2023 is between 19% and 25% depending on the level of the company's profits. Profits extracted from the company as salary or bonus are liable to income tax and also Class 1 NICs. However, salary and bonus payments and the associated employer's National Insurance are deductible in computing profits chargeable to corporation tax. There is no corporation tax deduction for dividends, which must be paid out of retained profits, but in the hands of the shareholder, they are tax-free to the extent that the dividend allowance is available and otherwise taxed at the relevant dividend rate of tax.

Gains realised by individuals are liable to capital gains tax, whereas a company pays corporation tax on chargeable gains.

All businesses with turnover of VATable goods and services above the VAT registration threshold, currently £85,000, must register for VAT. VAT-registered businesses must comply with the requirements of Making Tax Digital (MTD).

A sole trader and an individual partner in a partnership are self-employed and pay both Class 2 flat rate NICs and Class 4 contributions on their profits if their profits exceed the relevant profit thresholds. The payment of Class 2 NICs builds up entitlement to the state pension and certain contributory benefits.

Companies do not pay National Insurance on their profits but must pay employer contributions on payments of earnings made to employees.

By choosing the structure for your business, it is also possible to choose which taxes you pay – the taxes that are paid vary depending on the structure of the business.

It is important when choosing a structure to consider not only the current rates of tax, but also any future changes where these are known. The personal allowance is to be frozen at £12,570 until 6 April 2028, and the basic rate band is to remain at £37,700 for the same time period. The additional rate threshold is set at £125,140 for 2023/24 and will remain at this level until April 2028. The National Insurance thresholds are also frozen for this period.

The dividend allowance, set at £1,000 for 2023/24 is to fall to £500 for 2024/25.

The capital gains tax annual exempt amount, set at £6,000 for 2023/24, is to fall to £3,000 for 2024/25.

.

Choose Which Taxes You Pay

Richard wants to set up a business. Having considered the options, he decides that being a sole trader is the right decision for him.

Richard will pay income tax on any profits from his business. His income tax liability will depend on his total income from all sources. He will benefit from the personal allowance.

He will pay capital gains tax on any capital gains made from the sale of business assets, etc. where his net chargeable gains for the tax year exceed the annual exempt amount.

He will also pay flat rate Class 2 NICs and Class 4 contributions on his profits where his profits exceed the relevant thresholds.

If his turnover exceeds the VAT registration threshold, he must also register for VAT. If his turnover is below this level, he can register voluntarily as this will allow him to recover any VAT suffered, although he must also charge VAT on any VATable supplies that he makes.

3.   Take Advantage Of The Veil Of Incorporation

Sole traders have unlimited liability for any debts that their business incurs. By contrast, a shareholder is only liable for company debts up to the amount of any share capital that they own. Limited liability is one of the main advantages of choosing to run your business as a limited company rather than as a sole trader or partnership.

A limited company is a separate legal entity from its shareholders and directors. This is known as the veil of incorporation. The shareholders' and directors' personal assets are not available to meet the debts of the company. However, the money and assets of the company belong to the company rather than to the shareholders personally.

By contrast, where an individual operates a business as a sole trader, there is no legal distinction between his or her business and private affairs. This means that the individual is personally liable for any business debts.

Take Advantage Of The Veil Of Incorporation

Jack has set up in business as a limited company. He has 100 £1 shares that are fully paid up. He is the sole shareholder.

The business collapses with debts of £10,000. Jack is not personally liable for those debts. His liability is limited to his shareholding of £100.

4. Save Incorporation Costs

A limited company must be properly created in accordance with company law requirements and registered with Companies House. This process is known as incorporation.

Although a company formation agent, accountant, solicitor or chartered secretary can be used to incorporate the company in return for a fee, it is possible and relatively straightforward to set up the business yourself. Guidance on how to do this can be found on the GOV.UK website at www.gov.uk/limited-company-formation/register-your-company. A company can be registered online if it is limited by shares and it uses the standard article of association (also known as the 'model articles'). This service costs £12 and the company is normally registered within 24 hours. The same service can be used to register the company for corporation tax and to register for PAYE.

It is also possible to register a company by post using form IN01. The stated timescale for postal applications is 8 to 10 days and the service costs £40. A same day service is available as long as the application is at Companies House by 3 pm. This service costs £100.

However, you may wish to seek professional advice prior to setting up a company, particularly as regards to what is the appropriate share structure for your business to facilitate the tax-efficient extraction of profits (see Tip 5).

Save Incorporation Costs

Bill investigates the process of setting up a company for his new business. He wants to keep costs to a minimum and uses the online incorporation service offered on the GOV.UK website. This is straightforward to use and costs him only £12.

5.   Create Different Categories Of Shares In A Limited Company

One of the limitations of a limited company when it comes to setting an efficient profit extraction strategy is the need to pay dividends in proportion to shareholdings; dividends are declared 'per share'. To overcome this limitation, consider creating different classes of shares at the outset to allow the flexibility for different rights to be attributed to different shareholders. Because dividends must be paid out in proportion to shareholdings, creating different classes of shares makes it possible to declare a dividend for one class and not for another, or to declare different dividends for different classes of shares. This allows the flexibility to extract profits in a tax-efficient manner. A share structure of this nature is often referred to as an alphabet share structure, as the company can create A class shares for one shareholder, B class shares for another shareholder and so on.

Likewise, attaching different voting rights to different shares allows the decision-making to be vested in one person but for another person to receive a greater share of profits.

If an alphabet share structure is not created at the outset, it is possible to create different classes of shares at a later date, as long as this is permitted by the articles of association.

When using an alphabet share structure, it is sensible to plan ahead to ensure that the shares meet the conditions for business asset disposal relief (previously entrepreneurs' relief) (see Tip 98).

Create Different Categories Of Shares In A Limited Company

The Smith family are shareholders in their family company, Smith Ltd. Mr Smith holds 100 A class shares. These have full voting rights but no right to assets on a winding-up.

Mrs Smith has 100 B class shares. They have no voting rights and no right to assets on a winding-up.

Mr and Mrs Smith's sons, James and John, hold 50 C class shares each. They have no voting rights but have a right to a share of the assets on winding-up.

Having different classes of shares allows Mr Smith to retain full control over the decision-making and provides the flexibility to declare dividends for each class of share. This will enable profits to be extracted in a tax-efficient manner by tailoring dividends to utilise any unused dividend and personal allowances and basic rate bands. On a winding-up, the assets would be shared equally between the children.

6.   Keep Administration Costs Low

A sole trader is the simplest business structure to set up and run. It does not have the legal requirements associated with a limited company, nor is it necessary to agree the division of profits or losses as in a partnership or to negotiate a partnership agreement. There is no incorporation process, as there is for a company, and no need to file a confirmation statement and accounts with Companies House. Consequently, the administrative burden associated with being in business as a sole trader is currently considerably less than for a company.

However, a person operating as sole trader must notify HMRC of their self-employment and register for National Insurance. As with all businesses, records must be kept and tax returns filed.

A sole trader is also fully liable for any business debts.

7.   Keep All Business Profits For Yourself

An individual who is in business as a sole trader gets to keep all the profits made by his or her business. By contrast, profits made by a partnership are shared between the partners in accordance with the profit-sharing ratio. Any profits made by a limited company belong to the company and can be paid out to the directors/shareholders in the form of a salary, bonus or dividend (as appropriate) or retained in the company.

A sole trader is uniquely placed to enjoy all the benefits of his or her business success.

Keep All Business Profits For Yourself

Lucy is in business as a sole trader. She has a successful year and makes a profit of £100,000, which is treated solely as her income.

Her sisters, Katie and Emily, are in partnership, sharing profits equally. The partnership also makes a profit of £100,000. This is due mainly to a contract negotiated by Emily. However, the profits must be shared in accordance with the profit-sharing ratio and Katie and Emily are each allocated profit of £50,000.

In each case the profits are taxed as the income of the individual concerned.

8.   Maximise The Skill Base

For a business to be successful, a range of skills is needed. Where a person operates as a sole trader, they either need to possess those necessary skills or pay an expert, such as an accountant, to provide the skills that they lack.

A partnership offers the opportunity to bring together people with different skill sets in a business scenario. This can strengthen the business and increase the likelihood of success. Likewise, operating as a company offers the opportunity to recruit individuals to provide the full range of skills needed. Alternatively, skills that the directors/shareholders lack can be contracted out. In a personal or family company, it may be preferable and more cost-effective to contract out payroll and IT support, for example, than to provide it in-house. External experts can provide valuable support to a business, regardless of the way in which that business is structured.

9. Agree The Split Of Partnership Profits And Losses

The legal definition of a partnership is the relationship that subsists between persons carrying on a business in common with a view to profit.

In a simple partnership the partners share profits and losses in accordance with a pre-agreed profit-sharing ratio. A partnership is not a separate legal entity and partners are jointly and severally liable for the debts and losses of the partnership.

Normally, one would want the partnership agreement to be crystal clear on the split of profits. However, where the partnership comprises a husband and wife or civil partners, it may be advantageous to have a more loosely worded agreement to provide some flexibility in profit allocation to allow profits to be split in a way that minimises their combined tax liability. This could be achieved by a clause in the agreement which provides for profits to be determined in such a ratio as is agreed by the partners.

Agree The Split Of Partnership Profits And Losses

William and Ann are husband and wife and are in partnership together. As their other income fluctuates, they decide to keep the partnership agreement loose as to the share of profits and agree the split each year depending on their other income.

In year 1, William has other income of £20,000 and Ann has no other income. The profits of the partnership are £50,000 and are allocated £35,000 (70%) to Ann and £15,000 (30%) to William to equalise their total income and minimise tax liabilities.

In year 2, neither has any other income and profits from the partnership are £70,000. They agree to split the profits equally.

The absence of a set profit-sharing ratio in the agreement provides the flexibility to allocate profits in a tax-efficient manner.

In each case the profits are taxed as the income of the individual concerned.

10. Consider Purchasing An Existing Business

The failure rate among start-up businesses is very high. Instead of starting a new business, another option is to purchase an existing business. Although this may be more expensive initially, the success of the business is already proven, and the investment may be less risky in the long term. The aim of any business is to succeed commercially. It is also easier to attract finance for an established business than for a new start-up.

When buying an existing business, the purchaser can either buy the shares in the business (if the business is a limited company) or the assets in the business. Where the business is an unincorporated business, it will be the assets that are bought.

Professional advice should be sought prior to the acquisition of an existing business to ensure that the sale is structured in a tax-efficient manner and all legal requirements are met.

11. Run A Franchise

If you fancy being your own boss but have not had much previous business experience or are unsure whether your business idea will be successful, one option worth considering is running a franchise. Under a franchise arrangement the owner of a business (the franchisor) grants a licence to another person allowing them to use the business idea in a specific geographical location. The franchisee sells the franchisor's services or products under the franchisor's established brand name and receives help and business support. The franchisee pays an initial fee to the franchisor and also a percentage of profits.

Although it can be quite expensive to buy a franchise, the business is run on a proven model with an established name and identity, and support is available from the franchisor. Banks may also be more willing to lend to a franchise than to a new start-up.

Well-known franchises include Costa Coffee, McDonald's, Carphone Warehouse and Subway.

Chapter 2.
Finance And Investment

12. Prepare A Business Plan

A new business will need money when starting up to meet the costs of equipment, premises, stock, marketing, etc. A business that does not have adequate financing will fail.

It is important to identify how much finance is required and the preparation of a business plan is an important stage in this process. A business plan is a written document that describes the business, its aims and objectives and includes financial forecasts.

Preparing a business plan is a useful exercise as it forces one to think more carefully about the business idea and whether or not it has a realistic chance of success. It can help identify potential weaknesses and also gauge success.

The business plan is fundamental to external investors and they will make the decision about whether to lend money to the business on the strength of the business plan. Banks and other financial institutions will want to see a business plan before lending money to a new business.

There are various business plan templates on the internet which are available to download for free.

13. Choose The Right Finance Option For Your Business

It is important that the financing route chosen for a business is the right route for that business. There are many different sources of finance which are appropriate for different needs.

The sources of finance available to a new business include using your own money, borrowing money from family and friends, borrowing from a bank, attracting outside investors, borrowing from other commercial lenders and securing grant finance.

Different financing options will have different tax implications and these need to be considered.

It is advisable to take professional advice when seeking finance.

14. Secure Tax Relief On Loans To A Close Company

Tax relief is available for interest on loans where the money borrowed is used for certain qualifying purposes. Buying shares or lending money to a close company is a qualifying purpose, as long as the associated conditions are met.

A close company is one that is under the control of five or fewer participators or any number of participators if those participators are directors. Most family companies are close companies.

Relief is available for interest paid on a loan to buy ordinary shares in a close company or to lend money to a close company provided that certain conditions are met:

- you own 5% of the shares (either alone or together with associates); or

- you have some shares (not necessarily 5%) and work for the greater part of your time in the management of the company or that of an associated company.

It should be noted the availability of certain income tax reliefs is capped each year at the greater of 25% of income and £50,000. The cap applies to various reliefs, including relief for qualifying loan interest and loss relief.

Secure Tax Relief On Loans To A Close Company

XYZ Ltd is a family company. Leo owns 60% of the ordinary share capital and his wife Julia owns the remaining 40%.

Leo extends the mortgage on the family home, borrowing an additional £40,000 which he lends to the company.

As the borrowing is for a qualifying purpose, Leo is entitled to tax relief for the interest on the additional £40,000 of borrowings.

This is subject to the operation of the cap on income tax reliefs.

15. Borrow Money To Buy Partnership Assets And Obtain Tax Relief For Interest

Tax relief is available on money borrowed to buy equipment or machinery for use in a partnership, provided that the items in question qualify for capital allowances.

It may therefore be advisable to borrow money to buy equipment and machinery and to use savings for a non-qualifying purpose to maximise the tax relief available.

It should be noted that the availability of certain income tax reliefs is capped each year at the greater of £50,000 and 25% of income. Relief for qualifying loan interest is subject to the cap, which also applies to loss reliefs.

Borrow Money To Buy Partnership Assets And Obtain Tax Relief For Interest

Mo and Jake are in partnership as handymen and need to buy various tools for the partnership.

Mo has £2,000 of savings. He wants to buy the tools and also take his family on holiday but needs to borrow some money to do both.

He uses the savings to fund the holiday and takes out a £2,000 loan to buy the tools for the partnership. By using the savings to fund the holiday and the loan to fund the tools he is able to claim tax relief on the loan interest. If he had done it the other way round, he would be denied a deduction for the interest.

16. Beware The Return Of Funds Trap

As noted in Tip 14, relief is available on borrowings to fund a loan to a close company. However, relief is denied if the funds are returned to the borrower.

> ### Beware The Return Of Funds Trap
>
> Christopher is a director of a close company in which he owns 80% of the shares. Three years ago, he lent the company £50,000, funded from his savings.
>
> Christopher now wishes to extend his home and wants his money back. He knows that he can obtain interest relief for a loan to a company but not for a loan to extend his home. He therefore borrows £50,000 and lends it to the company so that the company can repay his original £50,000.
>
> However, he has fallen into the return of funds trap and interest relief is denied as the purpose of the loan is to return funds previously lent to the company to him.

17. Tax Relief For Business Borrowings

Interest paid on business loans or business overdrafts is a deductible expense as long as the loan is made wholly and exclusively for the purposes of the business. The incidental costs of loan finance are also deductible. It should be noted that where the business has opted to prepare accounts using the cash basis, the deduction for loan interest and finance costs is capped at £500. Unincorporated businesses with significant borrowings may therefore prefer to prepare accounts using the accruals basis to avoid the application of this cap. Where a business needs additional funds, borrowing those funds can be tax effective as a deduction is available for interest costs and also associated costs, such as any arrangement fee. This reduces the effective cost of the borrowing. It should be noted that the government is consulting on options to expand availability of the cash basis. Changes under consideration include increasing the interest restriction limit to £625, £750 or £1,000. The consultation runs from 15 March 2023 to 7 June 2023.

Tax Relief For Business Borrowings

PQR Ltd is a family company. The company wishes to expand its range of products and takes out a bank loan of £20,000 to fund the expansion. They are required to pay an arrangement fee of £500 in respect of the loan. Interest is charged at 6% per annum, giving an annual interest charge of £1,200 (£20,000 @ 6%).

The interest on the loan and the arrangement fee of £500 are deductible as an expense in computing the profits of the business. If the company pays corporation tax at 19%, the deduction is worth £95 in respect of the arrangement fee (£500 @ 19%) and £228 in respect of the interest (£1,200 @ 19%). The tax relief for the loan interest reduces the effective interest rate on the borrowings to 4.86% (((£1,200 – £228)/£20,000) x 100%).

However, if the company pays corporation tax at 25%, the deduction is in total worth £425 ((£500 @ 25%) + (£1,200 @ 25%)). The tax relief for the loan interest (£300) reduces the effective rate of interest on the borrowings to 4.50% (((£1,200 – £300)/£20,000) x 100%).

18. Attract Investment Under The Seed Enterprise Investment Scheme

Companies can consider using the Seed Enterprise Investment Scheme (SEIS) to raise money when starting to trade. Income tax and capital gains tax reinvestment relief is available to investors in the SEIS. The aim of the SEIS is to stimulate entrepreneurship.

The company can receive up to £250,000 in SEIS investment. However, a company which has already received investment through an Enterprise Investment Scheme (see Tip 19) or from a Venture Capital Trust (see Tip 20) cannot use the SEIS to raise finance. Any finance received under the SEIS counts towards the lifetime limit of funding from venture capital schemes of £12 million (£20 million for knowledge-intensive companies).

To qualify for SEIS investment, the company must meet certain conditions, be no more than three years old, have fewer than 25 full-time equivalent employees and have assets of less than £350,000.

In addition, the company must:

- carry out a qualifying trade;

- be established in the UK;

- not be traded on a recognised stock exchange at the time of the share issue;

- at the time of the share issue, have no arrangements in place to become a quoted company or the subsidiary of a quoted company;

- not control another company unless that company is a qualifying subsidiary; and

- not have been controlled by another company since the date of incorporation.

Tax reliefs are available to attract investors.

Income tax relief is available to investors who subscribe for shares in a qualifying SEIS company. Shares must be held for three years. Tax relief is given at a rate of 50%. The maximum annual investment is £200,000. Relief is not available if the investor is connected with the company.

Capital gains tax relief is available where gains are reinvested in qualifying SEIS shares. Relief is available for 50% of the reinvested gains. The relief is subject to the £200,000 investment cap.

Small higher risk companies that meet the requirements of the SEIS should consider using the SEIS to help them raise finance and attract investors.

Attract Investors Under The Seed Enterprise Investment Scheme

Big Ideas Ltd meets the conditions for the SEIS and is keen to attract investment.

Rick sells a painting in 2023/24, realising a gain of £60,000. He makes a qualifying investment of £60,000 in Big Ideas Ltd in the same tax year. As long as all the qualifying conditions are met, one half of the gain (i.e., £30,000) is exempt from capital gains tax.

19. Take Advantage Of The Enterprise Investment Scheme

The Enterprise Investment Scheme (EIS) is one of four venture capital schemes. It is designed to help smaller higher risk companies raise finance by offering a range of tax reliefs to investors. Under the scheme it is possible to raise up to £5 million a year (up to a maximum of £12 million from venture capital funds (EIS, Seed Enterprise Investment Scheme (SEIS), Venture Capital Trusts (VCTs), and social investment tax relief (SITR)) over the company's lifetime). Companies must receive investment from a venture capital scheme within seven years of its first commercial sale. SITR closed to new investment on 6 April 2023.

Higher limits apply to knowledge-intensive companies.

However, where the company is newly established, before using the EIS to raise finance, consideration should be given as to whether the Seed Enterprise Investment Scheme would be more appropriate (see Tip 18).

Under the EIS, tax relief is available to individuals who subscribe for shares in an EIS company. Income tax relief is given at a rate of 30% on the cost of the shares, subject to a maximum investment of £1 million per person per year (or £2 million per person per year where the excess of £1 million is invested in knowledge-intensive companies). The shares must be fully paid up. The income tax relief is therefore worth up to £300,000 to the investor. The investor can also benefit from capital gains tax and loss reliefs.

Although an individual connected with the company cannot generally obtain income tax relief on the purchase of shares, the EIS helps companies raise finance.

A company can use the EIS scheme to raise finance if:

- it has a permanent establishment in the UK;

- it is not trading on a recognised stock exchange at the time of the share issue and does not plan to do so;

- it does not control another company (other than a qualifying subsidiary);

- it is not controlled by another company or does not have more than 50% of its shares owned by another company; and

- it does not expect to close after completing a project or series of projects.

In addition, the company and any qualifying subsidiary must not have gross assets worth more than £15 million before any shares are issued and not more than £16 million immediately afterwards and have less than 250 full-time equivalent employees at the time that the shares are issued.

The company must also carry out a qualifying trade. Where the company is part of a group, the majority of the group's activities must be qualifying trades.

HMRC's Small Company Enterprise Centre can advise a company whether it meets the conditions for a qualifying EIS company.

Becoming an EIS company can help a company attract external investment.

20. Attract Investment From A Venture Capital Trust

The Venture Capital Trust (VCT) scheme was introduced to help smaller higher risk companies whose shares are not listed on a recognised stock exchange raise funds. To encourage investment, tax relief is given to investors. Income tax relief is given to investors at a rate of 30%. An investor can invest up to £200,000 a year in a VCT. Capital gains tax relief on disposal may also be available.

To attract VCT investment the company must meet certain conditions regarding its trading activities, its gross assets, its independence and its subsidiaries. The company must have no more than £15 million in gross assets, less than 250 employees and, at the time of receiving the investment, it must be less than seven years since its first commercial sale.

To qualify, a company must also:

- have a permanent establishment in the UK;

- carry out a qualifying trade;

- plan to spend the investment on a qualifying trade;

- not be listed on a recognised stock exchange at the time of the investment; and

- not be controlled by another company.

The maximum amount that can be raised is £5 million a year, subject to a lifetime limit of £12 million of investment from venture schemes. Higher limits apply to knowledge-intensive companies, which can raise up to £10 million per year and £20 million over their lifetime.

Companies that meet these requirements could consider tapping into VCT funding. Companies interested in raising investment from a venture capital scheme can seek advanced assurance that an investment would meet the conditions of the scheme. This can be beneficial in attracting investors.

Chapter 3.
Early Years

21. Register With HMRC And Avoid Penalties

22. Choose A 31 March Accounting Date

23. Choose Your Corporation Tax Payment Date

24. Consider Whether To Register For VAT Voluntarily

25. Cash Basis v Accruals Basis

26. Save Work By Joining The VAT Flat Rate Scheme

27. Limited Cost Businesses And The VAT Flat Rate Scheme

28. Carry Back Early Year Losses

29. Choose The Method Of Relief For Early Year Losses

30. Extend The Loss To Capital Gains

31. Consider Not Claiming Capital Allowances

32. Claim Relief For Pre-Trading Expenditure

33. Claim Relief For Capital Expenditure Incurred Before The Start Of Trading

21. Register With HMRC And Avoid Penalties

Regardless of whether you are running your business as a sole trader, a company or a partnership, you need to tell HMRC.

If you are a sole trader, you must register as self-employed for self-assessment and for National Insurance. This should be done by 5 October in the business's second tax year. HMRC may charge a penalty for a failure to register by this date. This is to allow the tax return for the first year of the business, due by 31 January after the end of the tax year where it is filed online, to be filed on time.

An individual can register as self-employed online. This can be done online on the GOV.UK website at www.gov.uk/log-in-file-self-assessment-tax-return/register-if-youre-self-employed. HMRC will set up records from the information provided. Where a person is a partner in a partnership, they will also need to register for self-assessment. To do this, they will need the partnership's ten-digit unique tax reference (UTR).

Registration can be done online: see www.gov.uk/log-in-file-self-assessment-tax-return/register-if-youre-a-partner-or-partnership. The partner who is the nominated partner for the partnership must register the partnership for tax.

If you run your business through a limited company, after you have registered your company with Companies House, you must register for corporation tax. This must be done within three months of starting to do business. You can register online (see www.gov.uk/limited-company-formation/set-up-your-companyfor-corporation-tax). To register, you will need your UTR number. This is a ten-digit number which is sent to you automatically once you have registered your company with Companies House. Any business where turnover exceeds the VAT registration threshold will also need to register for VAT (see Tip 24).

Failure to notify may trigger late notification penalties, or for VAT, a late registration penalty.

Register With HMRC And Avoid Penalties

DEF Ltd was dormant for some years following incorporation. The company becomes active and makes a taxable profit for the year to 31 May 2023 on which corporation tax of £4,000 is due. The company has not notified HMRC that it is active, nor has it told HMRC that it is liable to pay corporation tax or delivered a return within 12 months of the end of the accounting period.

A penalty is charged on the potential lost revenue of £4,000.

A late payment penalty will also be charged on corporation tax paid late.

By notifying on time, this could have been avoided.

22. Choose A 31 March Accounting Date

If you are starting a new business in 2023/24 and are operating as a sole trader or a partnership, you may wish to choose an accounting date of 31 March to make life simpler and save work going forward.

From 2024/25 profits will be assessed on a tax year basis (with 2023/24 being a transition year). Where the accounting date is other than 31 March (or 1 to 5 April), it is necessary to apportion profits from two accounting periods to arrive at the profits for the tax year. For example, where accounts are prepared to 31 December, the profits that will be assessed in 2024/25 are $9/12^{th}$ of the profits for the year to 31 December 2024 and $3/12^{th}$ of the profits to 31 December 2025. Further, to work out the profits assessable in 2024/25, the accounts to 31 December 2024 and those to 31 December 2025 are needed, creating time pressure to finalise the accounts for the later year.

This can be avoided by having a 31 March year end.

Note: an accounting date of 31 March is deemed to be equivalent to the tax year, as is a date between 1 and 5 of April.

Choose A 31 March Accounting Date

Holly starts in business as a sole trader on 1 January 2023.

To keep life simple, she chooses a 31 March accounting date. She prepares her first accounts for the 15 months to 31 March 2024.

In 2023/24 (which is a transition year under which the basis of assessment moves from the current year basis to the tax year basis), she is taxed on the profits for the year to 31 March 2024, less overlap relief in respect of the profits for the period from 1

April 2023 to 5 April 2023 which have been taxed twice. In 2024/25 she is taxed on the profits for the year to 31 March 2025, deemed to be equivalent to the profits of the tax year.

23. Choose Your Corporation Tax Payment Date

Corporation tax is generally payable nine months and one day after the end of the accounting period. By choosing your accounting date you also choose the date by which your corporation tax is due. Where a business is seasonal this provides the flexibility to choose a payment date where the company is relatively cash rich.

Choose Your Corporation Tax Payment Date

Zak provides gardening services through his company ZK Gardens Ltd. He is very busy during the summer months and quiet during the winter. By choosing a year end of, say, 31 October, his corporation tax will be due on 1 August, when his cash flow is good.

By contrast, if he chooses a year end of 31 March, his corporation tax will be due on 1 January, which falls during his quiet time when his cash flow is less healthy.

Choosing a 30 April accounting date would mean that his corporation tax will be due on 1 February. As this coincides with the self-assessment due date for his personal tax of 31 January, a different date may be preferable from a cash flow perspective.

24. Consider Whether To Register For VAT Voluntarily

A business must register for VAT if the VATable turnover in the previous 12 months is more than the VAT registration threshold (set at £85,000 until 31 March 2026 or it is expected that this threshold will be exceeded within the next 30 days. A business whose turnover is below this level does not have to register for VAT but may choose to register voluntarily. This will allow VAT suffered on purchases and expenses to be reclaimed. The VAT reclaimed may offset the burden of charging VAT and accounting for it to HMRC.

Where a company is registered for VAT, it must comply with the requirements of Making Tax Digital (MTD) for VAT. Under MTD for VAT, a business must keep digital records and file VAT returns using MTD-compatible software.

Consider Whether To Register For VAT Voluntarily

Simon has turnover of £30,000 a year. He does not need to register for VAT but chooses to do so. As a result, he is able to recover his input VAT. In the first year of VAT registration, he recovers input tax of £3,500, making voluntary registration worthwhile. He must comply with MTD for VAT.

25. Cash Basis v Accruals Basis

The accruals basis is the default basis of accounts preparation for traders. However, unincorporated traders who meet the eligibility tests can instead elect to prepare accounts under the cash basis.

Under the accruals basis (also known as the 'earnings basis'), income and expenditure are matched to the period to which they relate rather than being taken into account when the income is received or the expenditure paid. This means that it is necessary to take account of debtors and creditors and work out prepayments and accruals. Relief for capital expenditure is given in the form of capital allowances. The accruals basis is the default basis for traders in the absence of a cash basis election.

Under the cash basis, income is taken into account when it is received, and expenditure is taken into account when it is paid. There is no need to match income and expenditure to the period to which it relates. Where the cash basis is used, relief for capital expenditure is given as a deduction from profits unless the expenditure is of a type for which a deduction is specifically prohibited (see Tip 53). Under the cash basis, the amount that can be deducted in respect of interest and finance costs is capped at £500.

The cash basis is only an option for eligible traders. To qualify for the cash basis, the trader must have cash basis receipts of not more than £150,000. Once in the cash basis, a trader can remain in it as long as cash basis receipts are not more than £300,000. These limits are doubled for universal credit claimants. Traders wishing to use the cash basis must elect in their self-assessment tax return for it to apply. The cash basis can only be used by unincorporated businesses. Partnerships qualify as long as they comprise wholly of individuals; LLPs cannot use the cash basis.

Eligible traders should consider using the cash basis to simplify the calculation of their taxable profits. The cash basis also provides automatic relief for bad debts as income is not recognised until payment is received.

It should be noted that the government is consulting on proposals to extend eligibility of the cash basis. Policies under consideration include increasing the turnover restriction, making the cash basis the default basis for eligible businesses, increasing the interest restriction limit and reducing the constraints on loss relief. The consultation runs from 15 March 2023 to 7 June 2023.

Cash Basis v Accruals Basis

John is a sole trader and prepares accounts to 5 April each year. On 31 March 2023 he invoices a customer £180 for work done on 28 March 2023. The customer pays the bill on 10 April 2023. John ordered some parts for £300 on 21 March 2023, receiving an invoice dated that day. He paid the invoice on 18 April 2023.

Under the accruals basis, the invoice issued to the customer on 31 March 2023 would be taken into account in the year to 5 April 2023 as the work was done in the year to 5 April 2023, as would the expenditure on the goods purchased on 21 March 2023.

However, under the cash basis, the income would not be taken into account until 2023/24, as it was received in that year. Likewise, the expenditure on the parts would be taken into account in 2023/24 rather than 2022/23, as the payment date of 18 April 2023 falls in 2023/24.

26. Save Work By Joining The VAT Flat Rate Scheme

Smaller VAT-registered businesses can save a significant amount of work by joining the flat rate scheme. The scheme can be used by businesses that have taxable turnover of less than £150,000. Under the scheme, the VAT payable over to HMRC is calculated as a percentage of VAT-inclusive turnover. The percentage depends on the nature of the business (see www.gov.uk/vat-flat-rate-scheme/how-much-you-pay).

A discount of 1% on the flat rate percentage is given to businesses in their first year of VAT registration, saving them money.

Once a business has joined the scheme, it can remain in it even if turnover exceeds £150,000 in a year as long as total income, including VAT, is not more than £230,000 in a year.

Using the flat rate scheme removes the need to record separately the VAT charged on purchases, reducing the time spent doing the books. However, VAT must still be charged on sales within the scope of VAT and a VAT invoice issued on which VAT is shown separately.

However, if you are a limited cost business, the scheme may not be beneficial for you (see Tip 27).

Save Work By Joining The VAT Flat Rate Scheme

Betty starts up in business as a photographer. She registers for VAT and joins the flat rate scheme. She is not a limited cost business (see Tip 27).

In year 1, her VAT-inclusive turnover is £24,400 a quarter. The appropriate flat rate percentage is 11% but as she is in her first year of registration, she receives a discount of 1%. She must pay over VAT of £2,440 (£24,440 @ 10%) a quarter to HMRC.

In year 2, her VAT-inclusive turnover has increased to £26,000 a quarter. She no longer benefits from the discount and pays VAT over to HMRC of £2,860 (£26,000 @ 11%).

27. Limited Cost Businesses And The VAT Flat Rate Scheme

Businesses that are classed as 'limited cost businesses' have a higher flat rate percentage than that applicable for their business type. The VAT flat rate percentage for a limited cost business is 16.5%.

A business is a limited cost business if the amount that it spends on 'relevant goods' is either:

- less than 2% of the VAT flat rate turnover; or

- greater than 2% of the VAT flat rate turnover but less than £1,000 per year (£250 per quarter).

The VAT flat rate turnover is the turnover of the business inclusive of VAT.

Only 'relevant goods' are taken into account in applying the turnover test to determine if a business is a limited costs business. Relevant goods are goods used exclusively for the purposes of the business, but excluding:

- vehicle costs including fuel (unless the business is one operating in the transport sector using a vehicle that it owns or leases);

- food or drink for the proprietor or staff;

- capital expenditure on goods of any value;

- goods for resale, leasing, letting or hiring out where that is not the business's main business activity;

- goods for resale or to hire out, unless this is the business's main activity;

- goods forming promotional items, gifts or donations.

In VAT Notice 733, HMRC provide the examples of relevant goods including:

- stationery and office supplies;

- gas and electricity used exclusively for the business;

- fuel for a taxi owned by a taxi firm;

- stock for a shop;

- cleaning products to be used exclusively for the business;

- hair products used to provide hairdressing services;

- standard software;

- food to be used for meals for customers;

- goods provided by a subcontractor and itemised separately;

- goods brought without VAT being charged if not otherwise excluded.

HMRC also provide the following examples of goods that are not relevant goods:

- accountancy fees;

- advertising fees;

- items leased or hired to the business;

- goods not used exclusively for a business (such as the electricity to supply a home and an office located in a home);

- fuel for a car unless the business operates in the transport sector;

- electronic devices, such as laptops or mobile phones for use in the business (as these constitute capital expenditure);

- anything provided electronically, such as a downloaded magazine (as this is regarded as a service);

- software that is downloaded;

- bespoke software, even if not provided electronically;

- stamps and postage costs; and

- goods bought solely to meet the turnover test to prevent the business from being classed as a limited cost business if the quantity of goods is such that they cannot reasonably be used by the business.

- Where a business is a limited cost business, it pays VAT to HMRC at the rate of 16.5% of VAT-inclusive turnover. This is equivalent to 19.8% of net (VAT exclusive) turnover.

- Thus, a limited cost business pays virtually all the VAT it charges over to HMRC, with virtually no allowance for VAT incurred. Where the VAT incurred on items that are not relevant goods is significant, the business may be better off leaving the flat rate scheme and using traditional VAT accounting.

- Where this is the case, the business should evaluate whether the additional administration costs incurred as a result of coming out of the flat rate scheme and working out VAT in the normal way is justified in relation to the VAT saved.

Limited Costs Businesses And The VAT Flat Rate Scheme

Joe operates a consultancy business and is VAT registered. His turnover is £25,000 plus VAT (i.e., £30,000 inclusive of VAT).

His expenditure on relevant goods is £400 plus VAT. However, he also incurs expenditure of £7,000 plus VAT on non-relevant goods.

The VAT incurred on the relevant goods is £80 (20% of £400) and the VAT incurred on the non-relevant items is £1,400 (20% of £7,000).

Joe would meet the test for a limited cost trader and under the VAT flat rate scheme would pay VAT of £4,950 over to HMRC (£30,000 @ 16.5%).

However, if Joe came out of the flat rate scheme, he would only pay VAT of £3,520 (£5,000 – (£80 + £1400)). Joe is much better off outside the VAT flat rate scheme, as he is able to recover the VAT on non-relevant items, such as services.

28. Carry Back Early Year Losses

A business often makes losses in the early years of the trade. There is a special loss relief available to individuals (whether sole traders or partners in a partnership), which allows a loss made in the tax year in which the individual first carried on the trade or in any of the three succeeding years, to be relieved against total income of the preceding three tax years. The loss is relieved against an earlier year before a later year.

Carrying back the loss relieves the loss at the earliest opportunity and generates a tax repayment.

It should be noted relief for certain losses is capped each year at the greater of 25% of income and £50,000.

The cap applies to various types of loss relief and to relief for qualifying interest. In some cases, the operation of the cap may limit the amount of early years loss relief that can be obtained.

Further, if the cash basis is used, it is not possible to relieve losses sideways or to carry them back using early years loss relief.

See also Tip 29 for alternative ways to relieve a loss in the early years of a business.

Carry Back Early Year Losses

Jessica starts her business in 2023/24, making a loss in the first year of £15,000. She prepares her accounts using the accruals basis.

In 2020/21, she had total income of £70,000. In 2021/22 and 2022/23, she had income of £80,000 and £65,000 respectively.

Carrying the loss of £15,000 back three years and setting it against her total income for 2020/21 of £70,000 will reduce her income for that year to £55,000 (£70,000 – £15,000) and generate a tax repayment of £6,000 (£15,000 @ 40%) plus interest.

29. Choose The Method Of Relief For Early Year Losses

As noted in Tip 28, losses made in the opening years of a business can be carried back against the total income of the preceding three tax years. This option is only available where accounts are prepared using the accruals basis.

However, this is not the only option for relieving early year losses. The loss can also be set against other income for the year in which the loss was incurred or the previous tax year or carried forward against future trading profits. Again, sideways loss relief against other income is not available where accounts are prepared using the cash basis (the loss can only be carried forward and set against future profits of the same trade). In certain circumstances, relief can be extended to capital gains, but again this is only an option where accounts are prepared using the accruals basis.

The basic aim of loss relief planning is to obtain relief at the highest marginal rate of tax and earlier rather than later. The decision as to which route to take to relieve the loss will depend on the level of other income, expected future profits, income of previous years and the rates of tax in the years concerned. Care should also be taken to preserve personal allowances.

It should be noted that relief for losses and qualifying loan interest is subject to a cap, which is set at the greater of £50,000 and 25% of income.

Where the loss arises in a trade carried on by an individual or a partner in a non-active capacity, claims for sideways loss relief (setting off the loss against general income of the same or the preceding year) are capped at £25,000 a year.

The government is consulting on changes to the cash basis. The proposals under consideration include relaxing the restrictions on loss relief.

Choose The Method Of Relief For Early Year Losses

Jane starts her business on 1 January 2024 and makes a loss of £10,000 for 2023/24. She prepares accounts using the accruals basis.

She has other income of £30,000 in 2023/24 and had income of £8,000 in 2022/23. In 2020/21 and 2021/22 she had income of £5,000 and £6,000 respectively.

She secured a major contract in May 2024 and as a result expects her profits to be £100,000 in 2024/25.

Jane can relieve the loss against her other income of 2023/24 of £30,000, but she will only receive relief at the basic rate of 20%. However, if she carries the loss forward and sets it against the profits of £100,000 for 2024/25, she will receive relief at 40%. By choosing this option, utilising the loss saves her tax of £4,000, rather than the £2,000 that she would have saved if she had set it against other income of 2023/24.

It is not worthwhile utilising the special relief for losses in the early years and carrying the loss back to 2020/21 as her income for that year is offset by her personal allowance and carrying the loss back would be a waste of her personal allowance and would not generate a repayment of tax.

30. Extend The Loss To Capital Gains

If relief for a trading loss is claimed against other income for the current or previous tax year, the claim can be extended by election to capital gains tax if there is insufficient income in the year to fully utilise the loss. Again, this option is only available where accounts are prepared using the accruals basis.

This can be useful in some circumstances.

This relief allows an unused loss to be set against the chargeable gains for the year, reducing the capital gains tax payable for the year. However, the loss is set against gains before utilising the annual exemption and consequently a claim will not always be worthwhile. In this situation it is better to carry the loss forward against future trading profits than set it against any capital gains. However, with the reduction in the annual exempt amount to £6,000 for 2023/24 and to £3,000 for 2024/25, the scope for utilising this relief is increased.

Extend The Loss To Capital Gains

Paul makes a loss in 2023/24 of £25,000.

He has no other income in that year but makes a capital gain of £80,000 from the sale of shares.

He elects to extend the loss to capital gains. The loss is set against the capital gain of £80,000 saving him capital gains tax of £5,000 (£25,000 @ 20%).

As his remaining gains (£55,000, being the £80,000 gain less loss relief of £25,000) exceed the capital gains tax annual exempt amount of £6,000 for 2023/24, setting the loss against capital gains does not waste this exemption.

Setting the loss against the capital gain provides immediate relief for the loss

However, if Paul expects to make significant profits in future years, he may be able to obtain relief for the loss at a rate of 40% if he is a higher rate taxpayer by carrying the loss forward to set against future profits from the same trade. The loss would then be worth £10,000, rather than the £5,000 relief obtained by setting it against his capital gain.

Paul will need to evaluate the benefit of relief now at a lower rate against the possibility of relief in the future at a higher rate in deciding how best to use the loss.

31. Consider Not Claiming Capital Allowances

Capital allowances augment a loss. In certain circumstances it may be better not to claim the allowances as this may preserve personal allowances. This strategy will allow higher allowances to be claimed in later years when profits are higher.

Note: where the trader has elected to compute profits using the cash basis, claims for capital allowances are not in point (with exception of cars when simplified expenses are not used). Instead, capital expenditure is relieved under the cash basis capital expenditure rules.

Consider Not Claiming Capital Allowances

Polly makes a loss of £18,000 in 2023/24, the second year of her business. She prepares accounts using the accruals basis. The loss includes capital allowances of £8,000. She has other income of £22,000 in the same year.

By not claiming the capital allowances, the loss is reduced to £10,000. She can set the loss of £10,000 against her other income for 2023/24 of £22,000 without wasting her personal allowance (£12,570 for 2023/24). The loss reduces her income to £12,000, which is covered by her personal allowance of £12,570, leaving her with £570 of her personal allowance unused.

Had she claimed capital allowances, she would have wasted £8,570 (£12,570 – £4,000) of her personal allowance as all but £4,000 of her other income (£22,000 – £18,000) would have been covered by the loss.

By not claiming the capital allowances now, higher allowances will be available in future years when profits may be higher.

If Polly is married or in a civil partnership and her partner pays tax at the basic rate, she could consider using the marriage allowance to transfer 10% of her personal allowance (rounded up to the nearest £10) (£1,260 for 2023/24) to her partner, reducing her personal allowance to £11,310. She could then claim capital allowances of £690 to reduce her income from £12,000 to £11,310 to exactly match her reduced personal allowance.

The ability to tailor a capital allowances claim allows the individual to optimise their tax position.

32. Claim Relief For Pre-Trading Expenditure

It is likely that expenses will be incurred in setting up a business prior to the commencement of that business. The opportunity to claim relief for pre-trading expenditure should not be overlooked.

For income tax purposes, relief is available for pre-trading expenditure if:

- it was incurred within seven years of the start of the actual trade;

- had the expenditure been incurred after the commencement of the trade, it would have been allowed as a deduction; and

- it is not otherwise deductible in computing profits.

In deciding whether the expenditure would have been allowed as a deduction had it been incurred once trading commenced, normal rules apply – the business must satisfy the 'wholly and exclusively' rule (see Tip 34).

The pre-trading expenditure is treated as incurred on the first day of trading. Consequently, it is taken into account in computing the profits of the first accounting period.

Relief is similarly given for corporation tax purposes.

It should be noted that different rules apply to capital expenditure incurred before the start of the trade (see Tip 33) and also for reclaiming VAT on pre-registration supplies.

Claim Relief For Pre-Trading Expenditure

Benny starts trading as a sole trader on 1 October 2023. In preparation for the start of his business he incurs various costs that would have been deductible had they been incurred after trading commenced.

The pre-trading expenditure amounts to £2,750. This is treated as incurred on 1 October 2023 (the first day of trade) and deducted in computing his profits for 2023/24.

33. Claim Relief For Capital Expenditure Incurred Before The Start Of Trading

Relief for pre-trading expenditure (see Tip 32) does not extend to capital expenditure. However, similar rules allow capital expenditure to be treated as having been incurred on the first day on which trading begins.

The way in which relief for pre-trading capital expenditure is given will depend on whether the trader prepares accounts under the accruals basis or whether an election has been made to use the cash basis.

Under the accruals basis, capital allowances may be claimed and any expenditure qualifying for capital allowances is treated as if it had been incurred on the first day of trading. However, eligibility for first-year allowances and the annual investment allowance are determined by reference to the date on which the expenditure was actually incurred.

Where the trader has opted to use the cash basis (see Tip 25), relief for pre-trading capital expenditure is given as a deduction in computing profits, unless the capital expenditure is of a type for which a deduction is specifically disallowed (as is the case for land and cars). The deductible expenditure is treated as if it were incurred on the first day of trading. Capital allowances can be claimed under the cash basis in respect of cars, but only if simplified expenses (see Tip 37) are not being used to claim a deduction in respect of business expenses for the vehicles.

Claim Relief For Capital Expenditure Incurred Before The Start Of Trading

David starts trading on 1 July 2023 as a sole trader. He prepares accounts on the accruals basis. In preparation for trading, he spent £80,000 on plant and machinery in October 2022. The expenditure qualifies for the annual investment allowance and David receives a deduction of £80,000 against his 2023/24 profits. For capital allowance purposes, he is treated as having incurred the expenditure on 1 July 2023.

Lucy also starts trading on 1 July 2023. However, she elects to prepare accounts using the cash basis. In October 2022, she spent £10,000 on shelving. Under the cash basis capital expenditure rules (see Tip 53) she is able to claim a deduction in computing the profits for 2023/24 as if she had incurred the expenditure on 1 July 2023.

.

Chapter 4:
Deductions For Business Expenses

34. Claim A Deduction For All Allowable Business Expenses

Significant amounts of tax can be saved by ensuring that you claim a deduction for all allowable business expenses. Generally, these are expenses which are incurred in the course of earning profits for the business.

The general rule is that business expenses can be deducted when calculating taxable profit as long as they are incurred wholly and exclusively for the purposes of the business. Consequently, you cannot deduct private expenses when calculating your taxable business profits (but see Tip 35 for dual-purpose expenditure).

This test is less stringent than the corresponding test for deductibility of employees' expenses, which also requires that the expense was necessarily incurred in performing the duties of the employment. There is no requirement that it was necessary to incur a business expense for it to be deductible, only that it was incurred wholly and exclusively for business purposes.

Where accounts are prepared using the accruals basis, a deduction is not given for capital expenditure, for which capital allowances may be given instead (see Chapter 5).

Where the trader has elected to use the cash basis (see Tip 25), relief for capital expenditure is given in accordance with the cash basis capital expenditure rules (see Tip 53). These allow capital expenditure to be deducted when computing profits unless the capital expenditure is of a type for which such a deduction is specifically disallowed (as is the case for land and cars).

To ensure that deductible expenses are not overlooked, it is important that good records are kept, together with invoices and receipts.

Claim A Deduction For All Allowable Business Expenses

Judd has a small business, which he runs as a sole trader. For the year in question, he incurs business expenses of a revenue nature of £12,000. The expenses are incurred wholly and exclusively for the purposes of his business.

The business expenses are deducted from turnover in the calculation of his taxable profits.

Had he omitted to deduct the expenses he would have paid unnecessary tax. This would have cost him £2,400 (£12,000 @ 20%) if he is a basic rate taxpayer and £4,800 (£12,000 @ 40%) if he is a higher rate taxpayer. It is important that records are kept of all business expenses.

35. Claim A Deduction For The Business Element Of Dual-Purpose Expenses

Although you cannot claim a deduction for private expenditure when computing business profits, if costs are incurred for both business and private purposes, you can claim a deduction for the business proportion where this can be separately identified. This situation may arise where a person uses his or her car, computer or mobile phone for both business and private purposes.

The costs must be apportioned between the business and private elements on a just and reasonable basis. For example, an itemised phone bill could be used to identify business and private calls. Likewise, a mileage log could be maintained to identify the split between business and private travel in a car used for both purposes.

Claim a Deduction For The Business Element Of Dual-Purpose Expenses

Mark is a sole trader. He has a mobile phone that he uses both for business and private calls. He prepares accounts to 31 March each year.

In the year to 31 March 2024, his mobile phone bills came to £1,200. He works out that 90% of his calls are for business and the remaining 10% are personal.

Mark is able to claim a deduction of £1,080 (£1,200 @ 90%) when computing the taxable profits of his business.

36. Don't Overlook Common Expenses

Although all businesses are different and the expenses incurred will vary depending on the nature of the business, it is important to make sure that you don't overlook any expenses for which a deduction could be claimed.

Common business expenses include:

- accountancy costs;

- advertising;

- motor expenses;

- travel expenses;

- insurance;

- stationery and postage;

- power and water;

- rent;

- staff costs;

- bank charges;

- telephone costs;

- internet charges;

- cost of goods for resale; and

- packaging costs.

37. Use Mileage Rates To Save Work

If you are a sole trader or in partnership and you use a car, motorcycle or goods vehicle for the purposes of your trade, you can claim a deduction for the costs incurred in doing so. To save work and remove the need to keep detailed records of the actual costs incurred, you can opt to use simplified expenses to claim a statutory deduction by reference to a fixed rate per mile.

Simplified expenses can be used regardless of whether the trader prepares accounts using the cash basis or the accruals basis (see Tip 25). However, it is not possible to claim a deduction by reference to mileage rates if capital allowances have ever been claimed in respect of the vehicle. Also, a business using the cash basis is not allowed to claim a deduction calculated by reference to mileage rates for goods vehicles and motorcycles if the cost of acquiring them has been deducted in computing profits under the cash basis capital expenditure rules. This is because the rates include an element to reflect depreciation of the vehicle.

For 2023/24, the approved mileage rate for cars and vans is 45p per mile for the first 10,000 business miles and 25p per mile thereafter. The approved mileage rate for motorcycles is 24p per mile.

The mileage rate covers the cost of buying and maintaining the vehicle, and also depreciation. Consequently, where mileage rates are used, it is not possible to claim a further deduction for fuel costs, servicing and MOT and such like. However, a separate deduction can be claimed in respect of incidental costs incurred in connection with a particular journey, such as road tolls or the congestion charge. A deduction can also be claimed for the finance element where the vehicle is acquired under a hire purchase arrangement or finance lease.

You do not have to use the mileage rates for all vehicles. However, once you have chosen to use this method for a particular vehicle, you must continue to use this method as long as you use the vehicle for your business.

Use Mileage Rates To Save Work

Sarah is a sole trader. She uses her own car for business and private journeys. In the year to 31 March 2024, she undertook 14,000 business miles.

To save work, she claims a deduction based on the appropriate mileage rate of £5,500 when computing her taxable profits for the year to 31 March 2024.

The deduction is computed as follows:

10,000 miles@ 45p per mile = £4,500

4,000 miles @ 25p per mile = £1,000

Total deduction   = £5,500

38. Use Actual Costs Rather Than Fixed Rates

Although using fixed rates to calculate deductions saves a lot of work, if the costs actually incurred exceed the deduction allowed using the fixed rates it is beneficial to calculate the deduction by reference to the actual costs. However, on the downside, this will mean that records of actual costs will need to be kept. It is a question of balancing the additional work against the additional deduction that may be available.

Where mileage rates are not used to calculate the deduction in respect of a car, capital allowances may be available in respect of expenditure on the car.

Use Actual Costs Rather Than Fixed Rates

Polly has a top-of-the-range sports car which she uses for business purposes. She keeps a record of actual mileage and servicing costs for a year.

She undertakes 10,000 business miles and her actual costs are £6,000. If she claimed a fixed rate deduction by reference to mileage rates (see Tip 37) she would be entitled to a deduction of £4,500 (10,000 miles @ 45p per mile).

By basing the deduction on actual costs, she is able to enjoy a higher deduction, reducing profit and saving tax. The additional deduction of £1,500 saves tax of £600 assuming Polly is a higher rate taxpayer.

She can also claim capital allowances in respect of the capital expenditure on the car (making the necessary adjustment to reflect any private use).

39. Home Office: Deduction For Business Use (Fixed Costs)

Many small businesses are run from home and a proportion of the costs associated with running and maintaining a home can be deducted in computing the profits of the business.

The fixed costs associated with a home are incurred regardless of whether there is any business use of the property. These include rent, mortgage interest, insurance, council tax and general repairs.

Where a part of the house is set aside specifically for business use, a proportion of the fixed costs can be deducted in computing business profits. The apportionment should be made on a just and reasonable basis, such as by reference to floor area or the number of rooms.

However, where part of the home is used exclusively for business use, that part will not benefit from the capital gains tax main residence exemption when the property is sold and any gain apportioned to the business part will be taxable. In practice, though, this is rarely a problem as any taxable gain on the business part is usually covered by the capital gains tax annual exemption.

However, as the capital gains tax annual exemption falls (to £6,000 for 2023/24 and to £3,000 for 2024/25), it may be prudent not to use an area exclusively for business. For example, a room used as an office during the day could be used for homework by the trader's children in the evening.

Home Office: Deduction For Business Use (Fixed Costs)

Evie runs a small business from home. She uses one room exclusively for the purposes of her business. Her home has ten rooms.

For the year in question she pays home insurance of £300, rent of £12,000 and council tax of £1,500; a total of £13,800. She claims a deduction of 10%, i.e. £1,380, in computing her business profits.

40. Home Office: Deduction For Running Costs

The costs associated with a home comprise fixed costs (see Tip 39) and running costs. Running costs vary with use.

Where a business is run from home, a deduction is available for the additional running costs incurred as a result. This will include the cost of using additional electricity, water and gas, additional cleaning costs, etc.

If it is not possible to identify the additional amount incurred as a result of business use, the total bill will need to be apportioned between business and private use. The basis of apportionment should be reasonable. An apportionment based on hours worked or number of people using the property for business and private use may give a more accurate result than using floor area or the number of rooms.

See Tip 41 for claiming the alternative statutory deduction rather than a deduction based on actual costs.

Home Office: Deduction For Running Costs

Phil runs a business from the family home. The annual electricity bill is £2,000 and Phil determines that based on the hours worked, his business use accounts for 60% of the bill. He claims a deduction of £1,200.

41. Business Use Of Home: Fixed Deduction

Under the simplified expenses rules, a statutory deduction is available for business use of home. The statutory deduction can be used by sole traders and by partnerships. It is not available to companies. Consider using simplified expenses to claim a fixed rate reduction to save the work that is involved in working out a deduction based on actual costs.

You can claim a fixed deduction each month in respect of business use of your home. The amount of the deduction depends on the number of hours spent at home during that month working wholly and exclusively on the business (including any hours worked by employees). The fixed monthly deductions are as shown in the table below.

No. of hours worked at home in month	Monthly deduction
25 to 50	£10
51 to 100	£18
101 or more	£26

Business Use Of Home: Fixed Deduction

Nicola is self-employed as a beautician. She carries out treatments both at clients' houses and at her own home. She also undertakes the administration tasks associated with running the business at home. Each month she spends 60 hours working at home. She claims a fixed rate deduction by reference to the set amount of £18 per month.

This equates to an annual deduction of £216.

42. Business Premises Used As A Home: Statutory Disallowance

Where a trader lives in premises that are also the business premises (as may be the case, for example, for someone running a bed and breakfast or a boutique hotel), a deduction can be made for premises costs to the extent that they relate to the business when working out the taxable profits for the business. However, the costs relating to the private living accommodation must be disallowed.

To simplify matters, a fixed rate disallowance can be claimed where a trade is carried out at premises which are used mainly for the purposes of that trade, but which are also used as the person's home. Rather than having to work out the actual apportionment for home and business use, the private use disallowance is determined by reference to the number of people living in the premises. The private element is deducted from the actual total expenses to arrive at the allowable business deduction. The use of this fixed rate disallowance is available to sole traders and to partnerships.

The disallowance for the non-business element depends on the number of people who occupy the premises as a home (or otherwise than for the purposes of the business) and is computed on a monthly basis. The monthly disallowance for non-business use is as set out in the table below.

Number of occupants	Non-business element
1	£350
2	£500
3 or more	£650

To achieve the best possible deduction, the outcome obtained by using apportioned actual costs (Tips 39 and 40) should be compared to that obtained by reference to the statutory disallowance for private use. While using the fixed disallowance may save work, if the deduction calculated by reference to actual costs is higher, this will save more tax.

Business Premises Used As A Home: Statutory Disallowance

Elliott runs a bed and breakfast and lives on the premises with his wife. He runs the business as a sole trader.

In May 2023, he incurs premises expenses for the month of £2,000.

He claims a deduction for premises expenses by reference to the statutory disallowance.

The non-business element for two occupants is £500 per month. The business element is therefore £1,500 (£2,000 – £500) and he claims a deduction of £1,500 for the month.

43. Deduction For Uniform Or Protective Clothes

As a general rule, a deduction is not given for everyday clothes, even if these are only worn for business purposes. The wholly and exclusively test is not met as the clothes also provide warmth and decency. This rule means that, for example, a trader is not allowed a deduction for the costs of a normal business suit, shirts or jeans used exclusively for work.

However, a deduction is given for the cost of a uniform or protective clothes. A uniform may just be normal clothes which feature the business logo. By swapping your everyday sweatshirt for one featuring the business logo, the costs become deductible. The logo will have the added benefit of promoting the business.

Deduction For Uniform Or Protective Clothes

Jason is a self-employed personal trainer. He invests in personalised training kit featuring his business logo. By swapping his general sports gear for sports clothing featuring his business logo he is able to claim a deduction for his clothing costs.

44. Deduct Allowable Travel Expenses

Most businesses incur travel expenses and these can be significant. It is therefore important that you deduct allowable travel expenses when computing your profits.

The rules relating to travel expenses can be complicated, so consider taking advice to ensure you claim what you can and don't fall foul of the rules.

In the case of a sole trader or partnership, if the business is based away from home, the costs of travelling to the business base from home are not deductible. The costs of commuting are not allowable as these are incurred to put the person in a position to work rather than being incurred in running the business. However, if the business is based at home, the costs of travel from home to the premises of a customer or supplier are deductible.

Where the proprietor or partner uses his or her own car or van for work, the deduction may be based on a mileage rate (see Tip 37). If public transport is used, the deduction is the actual cost incurred. There is no requirement to take the cheapest mode of transport – so you can travel first class to a business meeting and claim the full deduction. The deduction hinges only on why the costs were incurred.

Where the business is run as a company, all travel costs met by the company are deductible in computing the company's profits. However, if the company meets the costs of private travel undertaken by an employee or a director (such as home-to-work travel costs), this may give rise to a benefit in kind tax charge on the recipient and a Class 1A National Insurance liability on the company.

It should be noted that tax relief is not given for home-to-work travel where a worker's services are provided to an engager through an employment intermediary (such as a personal service company or an umbrella company) and the worker is subject to the direction, supervision or control of the engager.

Deduct Allowable Travel Expenses

David runs a small business as a sole trader from a unit on a nearby business estate.

He drives to work each day. The costs of this journey cannot be deducted as an expense of the business.

He has regular meetings with suppliers. He drives from the office to the station and takes a train to the meeting, returning by train and car back to the office at the end of the day. The associated travel costs are deductible in computing the taxable profits of his business.

45. Claim A Deduction For Training Costs

A self-employed person may be able to claim a deduction for training costs.

However, a distinction is drawn between training to update existing skills and training to acquire a new skill. The former is treated as revenue expenditure and is deductible in computing the profits of the business, whereas the latter is regarded as capital expenditure which is not deductible as an expense.

Many professions require their members to undergo regular training to keep their skills up to date. These costs can be deducted in computing the profits, along with any associated travelling costs.

Claim A Deduction For Training Costs

Dermot is self-employed as a dentist. He attends a training course on the latest techniques. The course costs £2,000 and as the expenditure is treated as revenue rather than capital, it is deductible in computing his business profits.

46. Allowable Entertaining Costs

As a general rule, entertaining expenses are not deductible. However, there are some types of entertaining expenditure for which a deduction is allowed.

The main exception to the general rule is expenditure on the entertaining of employees, the costs of which can be deducted. However, depending on the nature of the entertaining, this may give rise to a benefit in kind taxable on the employee.

Promotional events are not treated as entertainment and the costs can be deducted. However, the cost of any food, drink or any other hospitality is not allowable.

Allowable Entertaining Costs

LMN Ltd is a family company.

The company holds a Christmas party each year, which is attended by staff and their partners.

The company can deduct the costs of holding the party in computing its business profits. This disallowance for entertaining does not apply to staff entertaining.

As long as the cost is less than £150 per head, the employees will not suffer a benefit in kind tax charge as the benefit will fall within the exemption for Christmas parties and similar functions.

47. Deduction For Business Gifts

Although business gifts are not deductible as a general rule, there is an exception for small gifts that carry a conspicuous advertisement for the trader, such as a branded diary, mouse mat or pen. However, for a deduction to be forthcoming, the gift must not be food, drink or tobacco. The cost of all gifts to the recipient in the tax year is capped at £50.

A deduction can also be claimed for the cost of free samples given to the public.

Deduction For Business Gifts

Roger is a self-employed gardener. He wants to give his customers a gift at Christmas. By giving them a diary featuring the logo of his business, he is able to claim a deduction for the cost of the gifts.

Had the diaries not been branded, the deduction would not have been allowed.

48. Obtain Relief For Bad Debts

Where the accruals basis is used, a deduction can be made for a bad or doubtful debt in the year in which the debt becomes bad or doubtful, or in a later year.

It is important to keep track of bad debts and to claim relief for any that become bad. If this is not done, the trader may end up paying tax on income that has not actually been received.

Where the cash basis is used, relief is given automatically for bad debts, as income is not recognised until it is received; consequently, where a bill is not paid, it is not taken into account as taxable income of the business. Therefore, there is no need to claim relief for bad debts if accounts are prepared under the cash basis.

By contrast, if accounts are prepared on the accruals basis, there is no automatic relief for bad debts. The income is recognised in the period in which the work is undertaken, regardless of whether the invoice has been paid. However, a deduction can be claimed when preparing the accounts for debts that are genuinely bad. Likewise, a provision can be made for doubtful debts.

Obtain Relief For Bad Debts

Josef is a builder. He carries out a job for a customer and invoices the customer £750. Josef prepares his accounts under the accruals basis and this invoice is included in his turnover.

The customer fails to pay the bill and Josef eventually discovers that the customer has been declared bankrupt.

Josef writes off the debt and claims a deduction of £750.

Jan is also a builder, but he elects to prepare his accounts under the cash basis. He invoices a customer £200 for a repair, but the customer moves away without paying the bill. As the income is never received, it is not taken into account in computing Jan's profits. As he uses the cash basis, the relief for the bad debt is given automatically.

49. Deduct The Cost Of Professional Subscriptions

Most professions require members to pay an annual subscription to a professional association for the right to use the qualification and designatory letters.

Where the taxpayer is self-employed, a deduction can be made in computing business profits for the cost of the professional subscription where the profits from that profession are assessed on the member. Subscriptions to local professional societies or branches are also deductible if the object of the branch or society is mainly professional.

Where the subscriptions are paid by a company, they are deductible in computing the profits of the company. As long as the subscription is on HMRC's list (List 3), the employee will not suffer a benefit in kind tax charge.

If the employee pays the fee initially and it is later reimbursed by the employer, the reimbursement will be tax-free as long as the employee would have been eligible for tax relief if they had met the cost personally.

Deduct The Cost Of Professional Subscriptions

Dinesh is a self-employed accountant. He is a member of the ICAEW and pays an annual membership fee of £700. He deducts this when computing the profits of his profession.

50. Deduct Incidental Costs Of Loan Finance

Many businesses need to secure finance at some point in their lifecycle, whether to fund the initial start-up or in order to grow the business. During the Covid-19 pandemic, many businesses may have needed to take out loans in order to survive. These may be in the form of Bounce Back Loans, loans made under the Coronavirus Business Interruption Loan Scheme and/or Recovery Loans offered under the Recovery Loan Scheme. A business may have taken out a bank loan to help them recover from the impact of the pandemic, or to build up or expand the business.

The incidental costs of acquiring finance can be deducted in computing the profits of the business and should be claimed. Costs which may be allowable include:

- legal and professional expenses associated with negotiating the loan and preparing the documents;

- underwriting commissions, brokerage and introduction fees;

- land registry fees;

- search fees;

- valuer's fees;

- commitment fees for making a loan available; and

- commission(s) for guaranteeing a loan.

However, it should be noted that where profits are computed on the cash basis, there is a general prohibition on the deduction of interest, apart from a £500 allowance. However, the £500 maximum applies both to the deduction of interest and any incidental costs of loan finance, capping the total deduction at £500.

The government is consulting on proposals to increase eligibility of the cash basis. The measures under consideration include relaxing the interest restriction by increasing the limit to £625, £750 or £1,000.

Deduct Incidental Costs Of Loan Finance

Hamish takes out a bank loan to fund the expansion of his business. He incurs professional fees of £500 in connection with the loan and pays an arrangement fee of £200. Hamish prepares accounts under the accruals basis.

He is able to deduct £700 in respect of these expenses when computing his business profits.

Had Hamish elected to prepare accounts under the cash basis, the total deduction for interest and the associated incidental costs of obtaining the finance would be capped at £500.

51.   Insure The Key Person

The success of the business may rest on one individual and insurance (key man insurance) may be taken out to protect against loss of profits resulting from the death, critical illness, accident or injury of that person. This may provide peace of mind.

As an added benefit, the premiums on such a policy are allowable in calculating the profits of a company or a partnership (but not a sole trader) if the sole purpose of taking out the insurance is to meet a loss of trading income arising from the loss of services of a key person, rather than protecting against a capital loss.

Insure The Key Person

Jack and Jill are directors and shareholders in the family company. Jack is responsible for generating the business and Jill undertakes the administration work.

The company takes out a key man insurance policy to protect against loss of profits should Jack be unable to work due to illness or death. The premiums are an allowable deduction.

However, had the policy been taken out to protect the value of the shares, the premiums would not be allowable.

52. Don't Be Tempted To Deduct Personal Items

There is something of a myth that if you have your own business, you can 'put expenses through the business' (and if the business is VAT registered, reclaim the input tax). This is very dangerous. Not only does it create extra work as these items need to be disallowed in the accounts, further, if they are left in as deductions, this may trigger enquiries into the accounts and possibly a tax investigation. Interest and penalties may be charged on the tax that is underpaid as a result.

Only expenses that relate wholly and exclusively to the business are allowable as a deduction against profits. Under no circumstances should private expenditure be treated as a business expense. The temptation to put private expenses through the business should be resisted at all costs. However, see Tip 35 for the allowable element in respect of items used for both business and private purposes.

The same applies for VAT. Under no circumstances should VAT on personal items be reclaimed.

Don't Be Tempted To Deduct Personal Items

Malcolm wants to undertake some DIY projects at home. He buys some materials and tools, which cost £480 plus VAT – a total cost of £576. He decides to 'put it through the business', claiming a deduction for the net cost of £480 when computing his business profits and reclaiming the associated VAT of £96 when completing his VAT return.

This is picked up in a compliance check by HMRC and Malcolm suffers penalties and interest on underpaid tax as a result.

Business and personal expenditure should always be kept separate, and any temptation to put personal expenses 'through the business' should be avoided.

Chapter 5.
Deductions For Capital Expenditure

53. Deduct Capital Expenditure Under Cash Basis

54. Obtain Relief For Capital Expenditure Under The Accruals Basis Via Capital Allowances

55. Capital Allowances Must Be Claimed

56. Obtain Immediate Relief For Capital Expenditure

57. Claim WDAs Instead Of AIA

58. Take Advantage Of Full Expensing For Companies

59. Claim The 50% FYA For Companies

60. Tailor Your Claim

61. Capital Allowances And Losses

62. Time Your Capital Expenditure To Accelerate Relief

63. Claim Capital Allowances For Mixed-Use Assets

64. Buy An Electric Car And Claim FYAs

65. Choose Lower Emission Cars For Higher Capital Allowances

66. Claim A FYA For Expenditure On An Electric Vehicle Charging Point

67. De-Pool Short Life Assets

68. Write Off Small Pools

53. Deduct Capital Expenditure Under Cash Basis

Where the cash basis applies, relief for capital expenditure is, in the main, given as a deduction in computing profits, rather than via the capital allowances system.

A deduction for capital expenditure is permitted under the cash basis rules unless the expenditure is of a type for which a deduction is specifically disallowed.

The limited disallowance covers capital expenditure on:

- an item of a capital nature incurred on, or in connection with, the acquisition or disposal of a business or a part of a business; and

- an item of a capital nature incurred on, or in connection with, education or training.

It also prohibits a deduction for expenditure on an item of a capital nature incurred on, or in connection with, the provision, alteration or disposal of:

- any asset that is not a depreciating asset (broadly, one with a useful life of more than 20 years);

- any asset that is not acquired or created for use on a continuing basis in the trade;

- a car;

- land;

- a non-qualifying intangible asset; or

- a financial asset.

However, while expenditure on a car cannot be deducted from profits, capital allowances can be claimed – but only if the simplified expenses system (see Tip 37) is not used.

The ability to deduct capital expenditure under the cash basis provides immediate relief for that expenditure in the period in which it is incurred. On the flip side, capital receipts are taken into account in computing profits where a deduction was given for the corresponding capital expenditure.

Deduct Capital Expenditure Under Cash Basis

Tony is a self-employed handyman. He uses a range of small tools in his job, which he replaces periodically. He opts to prepare his accounts using the cash basis. He prepares accounts to 31 March each year.

In the year to 31 March 2024, he spends £3,200 on new tools, the cost of which he deducts in computing his profits for that year.

54. Obtain Relief For Capital Expenditure Under The Accruals Basis Via Capital Allowances

The way in which relief is given for capital expenditure depends on whether accounts are being prepared under the cash basis or under the accruals basis. Where a cash basis election is made, relief for capital expenditure is given as a deduction in computing profits, unless the expenditure is of a type for which such a deduction is specifically disallowed (see Tip 53 for deducting capital expenditure under the cash basis).

Where taxable profit is computed under the accruals basis, expenditure on capital items cannot be deducted as an expense when computing taxable profits. Instead, relief for capital expenditure is given in the form of capital allowances. Plant and machinery capital allowances are available for a wide range of business assets, including cars, vans, computers, tools, machinery, equipment and furniture used in the business.

To claim capital allowances, the asset must be used wholly or partly for the purposes of the business and you must expect it to last at least two years.

There are different types of capital allowances.

The annual investment allowance (AIA) provides immediate relief for most types of plant and machinery (with the exception of cars) up to the annual AIA limit of £1 million, while writing down allowances provide relief over a longer period, at the rate of 18% or 6% depending on the type of asset. Some assets, such as new zero emission cars, are eligible for 100% first-year allowances (see Tip 64). Both companies and unincorporated businesses can benefit from the AIA.

For a limited period, companies are able to benefit from full expensing giving a 100% deduction for unlimited qualifying expenditure on new and unused assets that would otherwise qualify for main rate capital allowances where the expenditure is incurred between 1 April 2023 and 31 March 2026 (see Tip 58).

A 50% first-year allowance is available for expenditure by companies in the same period on new and unused assets that would otherwise qualify for special rate writing down allowances. This is available for expenditure incurred between 1 April 2021 and 31 March 2026 (see Tip 59).

All businesses that prepare accounts using the accruals basis are likely to have some capital expenditure that will qualify for capital allowances and the chance to obtain relief should not be overlooked

.

55. Capital Allowances Must Be Claimed

Capital allowances are not given automatically. They must be claimed, and they must be claimed within the time limit.

However, there is no requirement to claim capital expenses, or to claim them in the period in which the expenditure is incurred. Not claiming capital allowances, may, for example, be beneficial to prevent the personal allowance being wasted. Capital allowances can also be tailored. This may be beneficial for an unincorporated business to prevent personal allowances from being wasted.

A claim can be made in the tax return. This will be the self-assessment return for an individual, the partnership return for a partnership or the corporation tax return for a company.

The time limit by which capital allowances must be claimed depends on the nature of the business:

- Self-employed: 12 months after the 31 January deadline for filing the return.

- Partnership: 12 months after the 31 January deadline for filing the return.

- Company: 12 months after the filing date for the return for the accounting period to which the claim relates.

Capital Allowances Must Be Claimed

Elizabeth is a self-employed caterer. She prepares accounts to 31 March and purchases various items of catering equipment during the year to 31 March 2024 in respect of which capital allowances are claimed.

She claims the allowances in her 2023/24 tax return, which is filed by the filing deadline of 31 January 2025.

The deadline for claiming capital allowances for 2023/24 is 31 January 2026. This is 12 months from the filing date for the 2023/24 return of 31 January 2025.

56. Obtain Immediate Relief For Capital Expenditure

Businesses can claim immediate relief for capital expenditure on most items of plant and machinery by means of the annual investment allowance (AIA). The AIA can be claimed by unincorporated businesses (such as sole traders and partnerships) and by companies.

Capital expenditure up to the AIA limit qualifies for a 100% deduction against profits. The permanent level of the AIA is set at £1 million.

Once the AIA has been used up relief is given by means of the writing down allowance. The AIA is not compulsory. Writing down allowances can be claimed instead (see Tip 57).

The AIA cannot be claimed in respect of cars. However, a first-year allowance is available in respect of new zero emission cars (see Tip 64).

Note: companies may also be eligible for full expensing (see Tip 58) or a 50% first-year allowance (see Tip 59) for unlimited qualifying expenditure incurred no later than 31 March 2026. They should assess which claim is most beneficial.

Obtain Immediate Relief For Capital Expenditure

Luca spends £5,000 on computers, printers and other office equipment for his business. He claims the AIA and obtains immediate relief for his expenditure.

57. Claim WDAs Instead Of AIA

Although the annual investment allowance (AIA) gives immediate relief for capital expenditure, there may be circumstances when it is preferable to spread relief for the expenditure over several years and claim the writing down allowance (WDA) instead.

The WDA is an annual allowance that writes off unrelieved capital expenditure. Capital expenditure is generally allocated to one of two pools – a main rate pool and a special rate pool. The current rate of WDA is 18% for the main pool and 6% for the special rate pool.

The WDA is applied to the total of the written down value of the pool brought forward plus any capital expenditure in the period allocated to the pool, less any disposal proceeds.

It will be worthwhile claiming WDAs rather than the AIA if profits are low and claiming the AIA would create a loss which may not be relieved for some time. It may also be preferable to claim WDAs rather than the AIA if the asset is likely to be sold in the not-too-distant future, triggering balancing charges.

Claim WDAs Instead Of AIA

Harry is a sole trader. He prepared accounts to 31 March.

In May 2023 he incurs capital expenditure of £50,000 on plant and machinery. This is the only capital expenditure in the year to 31 March 2024. The written down value (WDV) brought forward on the main pool is £20,000. Prior to deduction of capital allowances, his profits are £30,000. He has no other income.

Although the expenditure is within the AIA limit for the year to 31 March 2024 and Harry could claim the AIA in full, this would turn the profit into a loss and he would waste his personal allowance for the year. Instead, he claims a WDA for the year of £12,600 (18% of £70,000, being WDV brought forward of £20,000 plus additional expenditure in-year of £50,000), preserving his personal allowance and spreading relief for the capital expenditure over a number of years.

Claiming the WDA reduces his profit to £17,400, of which £12,570 is covered by his personal allowance. Claiming the AIA would have created a loss of £20,000 and wasted his personal allowance for the year.

58. Take Advantage Of Full Expensing For Companies

For a limited period, companies are able to benefit from a deduction equal to 100% of qualifying expenditure without limit. Full expensing is not available to unincorporated business, such as sole traders and partnerships. Full expensing replaced the super-deduction which provided a deduction of 130% of the qualifying expenditure where this was incurred between 1 April 2021 and 31 March 2023.

Full expensing is available in respect of qualifying expenditure on new and unused assets that would otherwise be eligible for main rate (18%) writing down allowances (WDAs). To qualify, the expenditure must be incurred in the in the three-year period from 1 April 2023 to 31 March 2026. Expenditure on new computer equipment, office furniture, vans, lorries and machinery may qualify for the full expensing. However, the full expensing is not available for expenditure on cars.

Full expensing will be beneficial where the company's qualifying expenditure exceeds the annual investment allowance (AIA) limit. Qualifying expenditure eligible for the AIA is capped at the AIA limit of £1 million a year. There is no limit on the amount of capital expenditure that can be deducted in the period under full expensing.

A balancing charge will apply when the asset is sold. The calculation of the balancing charge will depend on the date on which the asset is sold.

Take Advantage Of Full Expensing For Companies

ABC Ltd is planning on investing in new and unused plant and machinery to boost their business. They plan to spend £5 million in the year to 31 March 2024. The expenditure would qualify for main rate WDAs at the rate of 18%.

The company has a number of options available to it as regards securing relief for its capital expenditure.

By taking advantage of full expensing, they are able to benefit from full relief for the expenditure of £5 million when calculating the profits for the year to 31 March 2024.

Under the AIA, they would only be able to claim immediate relief for £1 million of expenditure in the year to 31 March 2024.

The company could claim WDAs instead for all or some of the expenditure if this was felt to be more beneficial. This may be the case if they plan to sell the asset in a few years and want to prevent triggering a large balancing charge on the disposal of the asset.

59. Claim The 50% FYA For Companies

Full expensing (see Tip 58) is only available for qualifying expenditure by companies on new and unused assets incurred between 1 April 2023 and 31 March 2026 which would qualify for main rate writing down allowances (WDAs). Expenditure on new and unused assets in the same period that would qualify for special rate allowances, as would be the case for long-life assets, thermal insulation and integral features, is able to benefit from a 50% first-year allowance (FYA). Like full expensing, there is no limit on the amount of expenditure in the accounting period which is able to benefit from the 50% FYA. The FYA is not available for cars.

The allowance was originally introduced alongside the super-deduction in respect of qualifying expenditure eligible for special rate allowances which was incurred between 1 April 2021 and 31 March 2023. It was extended by three years to run alongside full expensing. As with full expensing, it is not available to unincorporated businesses; only companies can benefit.

The FYA offers a lower rate of deduction (at 50%) than that available where the annual investment allowance (AIA) is claimed (for which the deduction is 100%). However, where the AIA allowance has been used up, it will provide an opportunity to secure immediate write-off of 50% of the expenditure against profits – a more attractive option than a WDA of 6%.

Claim The 50% FYA For Companies

DEF Ltd prepares accounts to 31 March each year. They have already used up their AIA limit for the year.

They plan to incur qualifying expenditure on new thermal insulation in February 2024. The thermal insulation will cost £2 million.

They claim the 50% FYA, receiving relief for £1 million in calculating their taxable profits for the year to 31 March 2024. The remaining £1 million is allocated to the special rate pool and WDAs are claimed at the rate of 6%.

They will also be able to claim a WDA on the balance of the expenditure in future years, reducing their profits by a further £60,000 (£1 million @ 6%) a year, generating further corporation tax savings.

Had they simply claimed a WDA, they would have reduced their taxable profits by £120,000 in the year to 31 March 2024. By claiming the 50% FYA, they are able to reduce their profits by £1,000,000.

The corporation tax saving will depend on the rate at which the company pays corporation tax, which from 1 April 2023 is between 19% and 25%.

60. Tailor Your Claim

You can tailor your capital allowances claim to suit your circumstances. It is not a case of claiming either the annual investment allowance (AIA) or writing down allowances (WDAs), nor is it necessary to use up any remaining AIA balance before claiming WDAs on the balance. Further, there is generally no requirement to claim capital allowances at all.

By mixing the claims, you can claim the allowances that give the best tax result.

The options depend on whether your business is an unincorporated business or a company. Companies can also benefit from full expensing and a 50% FYA for unlimited qualifying expenditure (see Tips 58 and 59) – options that are not available to unincorporated businesses.

Tailor Your Claim

Adam is a sole trader.

In the year to 31 March 2024, he incurs capital expenditure of £20,000. He has a brought forward balance on the main rate pool of £5,000. His profit before the deduction of capital allowances is £26,000.

He claims an AIA of £13,430, reducing his profit to £12,570. This is the level of the personal allowance for 2023/24.

The remaining £6,570 of capital expenditure is allocated to the general pool. He could claim writing down allowances of £2,083 (18% x (£5,000 + £6,570)) but chooses instead not to claim WDAs for this year as doing so would waste some of his personal allowance.

After claiming an AIA of £13,430, the profit for the year is reduced to £12,570 (£26,000 – £13,430), which is offset exactly by Adam's personal allowance for 2023/24 of £12,570. Tailoring the claim allows Adam to preserve his full personal allowance for the year. He is able to benefit from the unclaimed WDAs in future years.

61. Capital Allowances And Losses

Capital allowances can create or augment a loss.

For a sole trader, if the loss is fully relievable without losing personal allowances, it may be worthwhile claiming capital allowances as this will save tax.

However, if claiming capital allowances will waste personal allowances it may be preferable not to claim them to preserve the personal allowance.

If the loss can only be relieved by carrying it forward against future profits, once again it may be preferable not to claim capital allowances as this will provide more flexibility going forward.

Capital Allowances And Losses

Joel, a sole trader, has a loss for the year to 31 March 2024 before taking account of capital allowances of £6,000. This is a loss for the 2023/24 tax year.

He has incurred capital expenditure in the year of £10,000.

He has no other income.

In the previous tax year (2022/23) he had income of £20,000.

He does not make a claim for the annual investment allowance (AIA). Instead, the capital expenditure is added to the pool, so that WDAs can be claimed in a later year.

He carries the loss back against the income of the previous year, reducing his income for that year to £14,000 and retaining his personal allowance for 2022/23 of £12,570. This leaves him with taxable income for the year of £1,430 and a small tax bill.

Had he claimed capital allowances (either AIA or WDA) he would have increased the loss carried back and wasted part of his personal allowance for 2022/23.

If he wanted to eliminate his tax liability for 2022/23 entirely, he could claim WDAs of £1,430. Doing this would increase the loss carried back to £7,430, reducing his taxable income for the year to £12,570, which exactly matches his personal allowance.

62. Time Your Capital Expenditure To Accelerate Relief

The timing of your capital expenditure around the year end will determine when relief is given and, where the AIA limit is exceeded, how relief is given. Bringing forward expenditure a few days around the year end will bring the relief forward 12 months.

However, where the business is an unincorporated business, if the AIA allowance has already been used up, it may be better to wait until the start of the new year so that you can claim the AIA for that year, rather than claiming the WDA.

For companies, the AIA limit does not pose a problem where the expenditure would otherwise qualify for main rate capital allowances as companies are able to benefit from full expensing on unlimited qualifying expenditure incurred in the period from 1 April 2023 to 31 March 2026 (see Tip 58). Companies can also benefit from a 50% FYA on unlimited qualifying expenditure that would otherwise qualify for special rate allowances as long as the expenditure is incurred before 1 April 2026.

Time Your Capital Expenditure To Accelerate Relief

James is a sole trader. He prepares accounts to 31 March.

He is investing in new computer equipment for his business. The equipment costs £10,000. If he incurs the expenditure on 2 April 2024 (which falls in the year to 31 March 2025), he will receive relief in 2024/25.

By accelerating it a few days to 28 March 2024 (which falls in the year to 31 March 2024), he will receive the relief in 2023/24.

Accelerating the expenditure by a few days brings the relief forward by one year.

63. Claim Capital Allowances For Mixed Use Assets

The fact that an asset is used both for business and private purposes does not mean that capital allowances are denied. Some relief can be claimed to reflect the business use of the asset. However, the personal element must be disallowed. For sole traders and partners where an asset is used for both business and private purposes, it is given its own pool to enable the disallowance in respect of the private use element to be calculated.

Where there is any business use of an asset, capital allowances can be claimed in respect of the business use.

Claim Capital Allowances For Mixed-Use Assets

Greg is a sole trader. He buys a new car for £20,000, which he uses for both business and private purposes. The car has CO_2 emissions of 40g/km and as such it qualifies for the writing down allowance at the rate of 18%.

The expenditure is incurred in the year to 31 March 2024.

The car is used 70% for business purposes and 30% for private use.

The WDA is £3,600 (£20,000 @ 18%).

This is reduced by 30% (£1,080) to reflect the private use.

Greg is therefore entitled to capital allowances of £2,520 for 2023/24 in respect of the car.

64. Buy An Electric Car And Claim FYAs

Cars do not qualify for the annual investment allowance (or for full expensing or the 50% FYA available to companies for a limited period). However, it is possible to obtain full relief for expenditure on a car in the year of purchase if you buy a new zero emission car that qualifies for a first-year allowance (FYA) of 100%. If the expenditure is incurred on or after 1 April 2021 and on or before 31 March 2025, a 100% FYA is available for new zero emission cars. Expenditure on cars with CO_2 emissions does not qualify for a FYA, only the writing down allowance (see Tip 65). WDAs are given at the main rate of 18% if the CO_2 emissions are between 1 and 50g/km and at the special rate of 6% if the CO_2 emissions are more than 50g/km.It should be noted that FYAs are only available for new and unused zero emission cars – second-hand electric cars do not qualify.

Buy An Electric Car And Claim FYAs

Gabby is a sole trader and prepares accounts to 31 March each year.

She wishes to buy a new car which she will use solely for business purposes. She buys a car in August 2023.

She chooses an electric car with zero emissions. The car costs £28,000.

As the car is a new car with zero emissions, she can claim the FYA and write off the full cost of the car against her profits for the year to 31 March 2024.

Greg is therefore entitled to capital allowances of £2,520 for 2023/24 in respect of the car.

65. Choose Lower Emission Cars For Higher Capital Allowances

Cars that do not qualify for first-year allowances (see Tip 64) or in respect of which the FYA is not claimed, instead qualify for a writing down allowance (WDA). The rate of WDA depends on whether the car is allocated to the main rate pool or the special rate pool, which in turn depends on its level of CO_2 emissions.

Where the expenditure is incurred on or after 1 April 2021 and on or before 31 March 2025, expenditure on cars is allocated to the main rate pool if the car's CO_2 emissions are 50g/km or less. Cars with CO_2 emissions above 50g/km are allocated to the special rate pool. As noted in Tip 64 a FYA may be claimed in respect of new cars with zero emissions.

Assets in the main rate pool attract a WDA of 18%, whereas those in the special rate pool attract a WDA of 6%. By choosing a car with emissions below the 50g/km threshold, a higher WDA is available, reducing taxable profits and saving tax in the short term.

**Choose Lower Emission Cars
For Higher Capital Allowances**

Brad is looking into buying a new car for his business. He is a sole trader.

The car he likes costs £30,000 and he is deciding between two different models, one with CO_2 emissions of 35g/km and one with CO_2 emissions of 90g/km. He plans to buy the car in September 2023

If he chooses the car with emissions of 35g/km he will receive a WDA of 18%. However, if he chooses a car with CO2 emissions of 90g/km, he will receive a WDA of 6%. In the first year, choosing the lower emission car will mean that Brad can claim a WDA of £5,400, as opposed to a WDA of £1,800 if he chooses the car with higher emissions.

Brad is a higher rate taxpayer. Choosing the lower emission car will save him £1,440 ((£5,400 – £1,800) @ 40%) in tax for that year. He will receive relief for his expenditure on the car over a shorter time period if he chooses the lower emission car.

66. Claim A FYA For Expenditure On An Electric Vehicle Charge Point

Qualifying expenditure on electric vehicle charge points qualifies for a 100% FYA if the expenditure is incurred on or before 31 March 2025 for corporation tax purposes and on or before 5 April 2025 for income tax purposes.

Claim A FYA For Expenditure On An Electric Vehicle Charge Point

XYZ Limited wants to encourage employees to make green car choices. They invest in a number of workplace chargers, incurring the expenditure in June 2023. They claim a 100% FYA for the expenditure in their accounts for the year to 31 March 2024, benefiting from immediate relief on the expenditure.

67. De-Pool Short Life Assets

Special rules apply to short life assets. If the expected useful life of the asset is no more than eight years from the end of the chargeable period in which the expenditure was incurred, an election can be made to treat the asset as a short life asset.

Where such an election is made, the asset is given its own pool. Writing down allowances are given at the main pool rate of 18%. When the asset is sold, balancing allowances or charges are determined by reference to the written down value of the single asset pool. If the asset has not been disposed of by the eighth anniversary of the end of the chargeable period in which it was acquired, the written down value (WDV) of the single asset pool is transferred to the main rate pool. A short life election could be considered if the AIA has been used up or to prevent a large balancing charge on disposal.

De-Pool Short Life Assets

Jessica has purchased new computer equipment for her business, which cost £2,000. She expects to keep the computer for three years. She does not wish to claim the AIA. She makes a short life asset election.

After two years the WDV on the pool is £1,345. The following year she sells the computer equipment for £800.

By making a short life asset election she is entitled to a balancing allowance of £545 (the value of the single asset pool of £1,345 less the sale proceeds of £800) on disposal.

120

Without the election, the disposal proceeds would have been swallowed up by the main rate pool. Had the AIA been claimed, a balancing charge of £800 would have arisen on the sale.

68. Write Off Small Pools

Once the balance on the main rate or special rate pool drops below £1,000, you can write off the whole balance by claiming the small pools allowance. This saves the need to make on-going claims for small allowances and also accelerates the relief.

Write Off Small Pools

Craig runs a small business. At the start of the chargeable period, the written down value on the main pool is £950. As this is less than £1,000, he can claim the small pools allowance and write off the remaining balance of £950 in full. He therefore obtains immediate relief for the pool balance.

Had he not claimed the small pools allowance, he would have been entitled to a WDA of £171.

Chapter 6.
Extracting Profits From A Family Company

69. Pay A Small Salary To Preserve State Pension Entitlement

70. Optimal Salary Where EA Not Available

71. Optimal Salary Where The EA Is Available

72. Preserving The EA

73. Optimal Salary For Under 21s

74. Remuneration Or Dividend?

75. Utilise The Dividend Allowance

76. Extraction Or Accumulation?

77. Impact Of Corporation Tax Rate On Distributable Profits

78. Use An Alphabet Share Structure

79. Timing Of Dividends

80. Anticipated Profits

81. Bonus Or Salary To Meet Living Costs?

82. Loss Making Companies

83. Employing Family Members

84. Beware The NLW and NMW Trap

85. Pay Pension Contributions

69. Pay A Small Salary To Preserve State Pension Entitlement

Entitlement to the state pension and contributory benefits is contingent on having paid or been credited with sufficient NICs. A person needs 35 qualifying years in order to secure entitlement to the full single-tier state pension, and at least ten years for a reduced pension. Fortunately, it is possible to achieve a qualifying year for zero cost.

Persons with earnings between the lower earnings limit (£123 per week; £533 per month; £6,396 per year for 2023/24) and the primary threshold are treated as paying NICs at a zero rate. The primary threshold is set at £242 per week (£1,048 per month; £12,570 per year) for 2023/24. These notional contributions preserve entitlement to the state pension and contributory benefits.

For 2023/24 the primary and secondary thresholds are not aligned. The secondary threshold is set at £175 per week (£758 per month; £9,100 per year).

For 2023/24, setting the salary between £6,396 and £12,570 will ensure that the year is a qualifying year for state pension purposes for zero NIC cost to the employee. As the personal allowance is aligned with the primary threshold (at £12,570) for 2023/24, PAYE tax should not be due either unless the personal allowance has been utilised elsewhere.

However, where the director/employee is aged 21 or over (and none of the other higher secondary thresholds apply), secondary contributions will be payable at 13.8% on earnings above £175 per week (£758 per month; £9,100 a year), unless the employment allowance is available. If a salary is paid to a director equal to the primary threshold of £12,570 for 2023/24, secondary Class 1 National Insurance of £478.86 will be payable (13.8%

(£12,570 – £9,100)). However, like salary payments, payments of secondary Class 1 NICs are deductible in working out the employer's taxable profits.

Paying a salary of between £6,396 and £9,100 a year will secure a qualifying year for state pension and contributory benefit purposes without any associated National Insurance costs for either the employee/director or the employer. However, it can be beneficial to pay a higher salary equal to the primary threshold/personal allowance (see Tips 70 and 71). Remember, directors have an annual earnings period for National Insurance.

Under real time information (RTI), details of the amount paid to the employee/director must be reported to HMRC electronically. HMRC's free Basic PAYE Tools software package can be used for this purpose.

Pay A Small Salary To Preserve State Pension Entitlement

Ian and Caroline are directors of their family company. To preserve entitlement to the state pension and contributory benefits they decide to pay themselves a salary of £9,000.

As this is between the lower earnings limit (£6,396 per year for 2023/24) and the annual primary threshold (£12,570 for 2023/24) they get the benefit of notional NICs but do not have to pay any actual employee contributions. As it is also below the secondary threshold of £9,100 per year for 2023/24, no employer contributions are payable either.

While paying a salary at this level is sufficient to ensure that the year is a qualifying year for state pension purposes, from a tax perspective, it may be worth paying a higher salary – see Tips 70 and 71 for details.

70. Optimal Salary Where EA Not Available

For 2023/24, the secondary threshold (£175 per week; £758 per month; £9,100 per year) is below the level of the primary threshold (£242 per week; £1,048 per month; £12,570 per year). This means that if a salary is paid that is equal to the primary threshold, there will be a small amount of employer's (secondary) Class 1 National Insurance to pay if the National Insurance employment allowance (EA) is not available and none of the upper secondary thresholds apply.

The EA is an allowance that employers can claim to set against the secondary Class 1 NICs that they pay over to HMRC. The allowance is set at £5,000 for 2023/24 (capped at the employer's secondary Class 1 National Insurance liability for the year where this is lower).

The EA is only available if the secondary Class 1 NIC liability for 2022/23 was less than £100,000. The EA is not available for companies where the sole employee is also a director; consequently, it is not available for most personal companies.

Where the EA is not available, it is possible for 2023/24 to pay a salary equal to the secondary threshold of £9,100 without paying any National Insurance (employee's or employer's) or, assuming that the personal allowance (set at £12,570 for 2023/24) is not used up elsewhere, any personal tax. Thus, the maximum salary that can be paid free of tax and National Insurance in 2023/24 is £9,100. If the employer does not want the bother of paying employer's National Insurance over to HMRC, the company may choose to set the salary at £9,100 for 2023/24 where the EA is not available.

However, as both salary and the associated employer's National Insurance are deductible in computing taxable profits for corporation tax, the optimal salary for 2023/24 is one equal to £12,570 (the level of the primary threshold and the personal allowance). The corporation tax saving on the additional salary and employer's NIC (at a rate of at least 19%) outweighs the employer's National Insurance payable.

Optimal Salary Where EA Not Available

Flo operates a personal company. She does not want to be bothered with the admin of paying National Insurance over to HMRC, so the company pays her a salary equal to the secondary threshold of £9,100 for 2023/24. She is not entitled to the EA as she is the sole employee and a director.

Fiona likes to save as much tax as she can. She too is the sole employee and the director of her personal company, and not entitled to the EA. For 2023/24, her company pays her a salary of £12,570, taking the employer's National Insurance hit to benefit from higher corporation tax deductions to lower her overall tax bill.

71. Optimal Salary Where The EA Is Available

Eligible employers are able to claim an employment allowance (EA) of up to £5,000 a year for 2023/24 which reduces the amount of employer's Class 1 NIC that they pay. However, the allowance is not available to companies where the sole employee is also a director. This is the case for many personal service companies (but see Tip 70 for the optimal salary where the EA is not available and Tip 72 on preserving entitlement to the EA). However, most family companies are eligible to claim the allowance.

Where the EA is available and not fully utilised against secondary NIC payable in respect of other employees' earnings, it is possible to pay a salary equal to the personal allowance (set at £12,570 for 2023/24) free of tax and National Insurance. The employer's National Insurance that would otherwise be due to the extent that the salary exceeds the secondary threshold of £9,100 is sheltered by the EA.

However, once the salary reaches the level of the personal allowance and primary threshold, any further salary will attract income tax at 20% and employee's National Insurance at 12%. The combined tax and employee's National Insurance hit outweighs the associated corporation tax relief. Consequently, it is more efficient to extract further profits as dividends.

It should be noted, however, where the employee is not a director, he or she must be paid at least the National Living Wage (if aged 23 or over), set at £10.42 per hour from 1 April 2023, or the National Minimum Wage appropriate to their age if the employee is under the age of 23.

A person who is not a director does not have an annual earnings period and must pay primary National Insurance by reference to the thresholds applying at the time that the payment is made. For 2023/24, the primary threshold is £242 per week (£1,048 per month).

Where one of the upper secondary thresholds applies, it is possible to pay a higher salary free of employer's National Insurance. See Tip 73 for the impact that this has on setting the salary level.

Optimal Salary Where The EA Is Available

Susan is the director in her family company. She is 35. For 2023/24 she pays herself a salary equal to her personal allowance of £12,570. Her husband John is also employed in the company.

As the salary paid is equal to the primary threshold, Susan pays no employee NICs on her salary.

In the absence of the NIC EA, the company would pay employer NIC of £478.86 ((£12,570 – £9,100) @ 13.8%).

However, as the company has at least one other employee and the EA is available, the employer's NIC would be offset by the EA of £5,000, such that no actual employer's NIC is payable until the EA is used up.

It is not beneficial to pay a higher salary as once the personal allowance and primary threshold are exceeded, Susan will pay tax at 20% and employee's National Insurance at 12% on the excess. This will outweigh the corporation tax saving on the higher salary, which is deductible in computing the company's taxable profits.

72. Preserving The EA

The National Insurance employment allowance (EA) (set at £5,000 for 2023/24) is not available where the company only has one employee and that employee is also a director. This may be the case for a personal company with a single director and employee.

As noted at Tip 71, where the EA is available, it is possible to pay a salary equal to the personal allowance (£12,570 for 2023/24) free of tax and National Insurance. To ensure that the EA remains available, a company must have more than one employee, or if the company only has one employee, that employee must not also be a director.

Personal companies where the sole employee is also the director who wish to retain entitlement to the EA could consider employing another person, maybe a family member, or resigning as a director and appointing another person (perhaps a spouse, civil partner or other family member) as a director instead.

As noted in Tip 70, where the EA is not available, the optimal salary remains at £12,570 as the small amount of employer's National Insurance payable is more than offset by the corporation tax deduction on the additional salary and the employer's National Insurance.

Preserving The EA

Hayley is setting up a personal company, H Ltd, and was intending to be the director and sole employee.

However, after speaking to her accountant as regards optimal profit extraction strategies, she decides not to be a director, appointing her husband as the director instead.

Although Hayley is the sole employee, as she is not a director, H Ltd is able to claim the EA. Consequently, the company can pay her a salary of £12,570 (equal to her personal allowance and primary threshold for 2023/24) free of tax and National Insurance.

73. Optimal Salary For Under 21s

A higher secondary threshold applies where an employee is under the age of 21.

No employer's National Insurance is payable on an employee's (or director's) earnings where the employee is under the age of 21 until the employee's earnings exceed the employer's upper secondary threshold for under 21s, set at £967 per week (£4,189 per month; £50,270 per year) for 2023/24.

This means that where the director or employee is under 21 (for example, in a family company, maybe one or more of the director's children) the optimal salary for 2023/24 is equivalent to the personal allowance of £12,570 (assuming that this is not utilised elsewhere). It does not matter whether the employment allowance (EA) is available or not. A salary at this level can be paid free of tax and National Insurance.

Note: Care should be taken that the salary paid to the family member reflects the work done, to preserve the corporation tax deduction, and also that if the recipient is not a director, they are paid at least the National Minimum Wage for their age.

Optimal Salary For Under 21s

The Brown family run their own family company; Brown Ltd. Mr Brown is the sole director. His wife and his daughter Charlotte, who is 19, are employed part-time by the company. He also employs a number of other employees and the EA is fully utilised.

As his daughter Charlotte is under 21, it is beneficial to the family to pay her a salary of £12,570, as no employer's National Insurance is payable as her earnings are below the upper secondary threshold for under 21s (£50,270 per year for 2023/24). This is equivalent to a salary of £1,048 per month. The salary can be paid free of tax and National Insurance.

74.   Remuneration Or Dividend?

One of the perceived major benefits of incorporation is the ability to extract profits from the company by way of dividends. The main advantage is the National Insurance saving, as no NICs are payable on dividends, whereas a salary payment would attract employee NICs of 12% (or 2% once the upper earnings limit has been reached) and employer NICs of 13.8% (2023/24 figures) once the salary exceeds the primary and secondary thresholds.

All taxpayers receive a dividend 'allowance', regardless of their marginal rate of tax. This dividend allowance is set at £1,000 for 2023/24, having been reduced from £2,000 which applied for the 2022/23 tax year. It is set to fall again to £500, for 2024/25. This reduces the ability to extract profits as dividends free of further tax.

The dividend allowance is not an 'allowance' as such, rather it is a zero-rate band which taxes the first £1,000 of taxable dividend income at a rate of 0%. Thereafter, for 2023/24 dividends (which are treated as the top slice of taxable income) are taxed at 8.75% to the extent that they fall within the basic rate band, 33.75% to the extent that they fall with the higher rate band and 39.35% to the extent that they fall within the additional rate band.

A payment of salary will attract tax at the taxpayer's marginal rate of income tax (20%, 40% or 45% (or, for Scottish taxpayers, at the relevant Scottish rate)). Salary payments are deductible in calculating profit for corporation tax purposes, unlike dividends which must be paid out of after-tax profits. Further, a dividend can only be paid if there are sufficient retained profits. In addition, various company law requirements must be met.

It is not simply a case that dividends are always best, although in many cases, taking dividends will result in less tax and National Insurance than taking a salary payment. However, it must be remembered that dividends have already suffered corporation tax, which from 1 April 2023 is at a rate of between 19% and 25% depending on the level of the company's profits.

The best result will depend on the circumstances, as the decision whether to take salary or dividends will depend on the interaction of various factors – respective rates of income tax, corporation tax and NIC, any other income that the taxpayer has and whether the company has sufficient retained profits.

To decide whether to extract profits by way of a dividend or a salary, crunch the numbers first. (The rates applying for 2023/24 and the financial year 2023are used in the example.)

Remuneration Or Dividend?

Paul is the director of a small company. He has profits of £20,000 (before corporation tax) and wants to know whether to extract them by way of a salary or a dividend. It is assumed that he has already received a small salary equal to his personal allowance.

He has a small number of employees and has utilised the NIC employment allowance in respect of employer's NIC payable in respect of earnings paid to his employees.

Via salary

Profits   £20,000

Less employer's NIC @13.8% (£2,425)

Available to pay as salary   £17,575

Less income tax @ 20%   (£3,515)

136

Less NIC @ 12%(£2,109)

Retained by shareholder   £11,951

There is no corporation tax to pay as taxable profits are reduced to nil after deducting salary of £17,575 and employer's NIC on that salary of £2,425.

Via dividend

Profits   £20,000

Less corporation tax @ 19% (£3,800)

Distributed as a dividend   £16,200

Income tax   (£1,330)

Retained by shareholder   £14,870

The whole dividend falls within the basic rate band (£37,700 for 2023/24). The first £1,000 of the dividend is taxed at 0% and the remaining £15,200 is taxed at 8.75%. The total tax payable on the dividend is therefore £1,330 ((£1,000 @ 0%) + (£15,200 @ 8.75%)).

In this situation, Paul is better off by paying a dividend as he is able to retain £14,870 of the profits, as compared to retaining only £11,951 if they are extracted by way of a salary payment.

75. Utilise The Dividend Allowance

All individuals, regardless of the rate at which they pay income tax, are entitled to a dividend allowance. The dividend allowance is set at £1,000 for 2023/24. The dividend allowance is being reduced. It was cut from £2,000 for 2022/23 to £1,000 for 2023/24 and will fall to £500 for 2024/25.

The 'allowance' is not an allowance as such, rather a zero-rate band under which the first £1,000 of taxable dividend income is taxed at a rate of 0%. This allows all taxpayers, even those paying tax at the higher or additional rates, to receive £1,000 of dividend income in the tax year, tax-free.

This provides the opportunity to make a spouse or civil partner a shareholder in a personal or family company and take advantage of their dividend allowance to extract an additional £1,000 of post-tax profits, free of tax.

As dividends must be paid in proportion to shareholdings, using an alphabet share structure provides the flexibility to declare different dividends for different shareholders. The reduction in the dividend allowance reduces the opportunity to extract profits free of further tax. However, an alphabet share structure provides the flexibility to pay dividends to also utilise family members' unused basic rate bands.

Note: the dividend allowance is reduced to £500 for 2024/25.

Utilise The Dividend Allowance

Ann has her own company. She is married and her husband John is a marketing director with a salary of £80,000. Ann holds 100 ordinary shares and John holds 100 A ordinary shares.

By declaring a dividend of £1,000 for A ordinary shareholders, it is possible to utilise John's dividend allowance and extract profits from the company without any further income tax liability. Assuming Ann has already received dividends to utilise her allowance, paying £1,000 of dividends to John instead of further dividends to Ann will save tax at either 8.75% if Ann is a basic rate taxpayer (a saving of £87.50) or at 33.75% (a saving of £337.50) if Ann is a higher rate taxpayer.

The same approach can be adopted in relation to other family members to ensure that the benefit of their dividend allowance is not wasted and to enable more post-tax profits to be extracted free of further tax.

By having different categories of shares for each shareholder it is possible to overcome the restriction that shares must be paid in proportion to the shareholding and to tailor the dividends to the circumstances of the individual.

76. Extraction Or Accumulation?

Before deciding how to extract profits, it is first necessary to decide whether to extract profits or to retain them in the company.

Retaining profits will mean that they suffer only a corporation tax charge. Whereas, if profits are extracted, they may suffer income tax and, depending on how they are extracted, NICs.

For the financial year that started on 1 April 2023, the rate of corporation tax depends on the level of the company's profits. Where a company has no associated companies, the rate is 19% if profits do not exceed £50,000 and 25% where profits exceed £250,000. Between £50,000 and £250,000, corporation tax is charged at a rate of 25% less marginal relief. The effect of marginal relief is that the company's effective rate of tax increases from 19% to 25% as profits increase from £50,000 to £250,000. However, due to the gradual increase, the marginal rate of tax in the marginal relief zone is 26.5%. If the company has associated companies, the limits of £50,000 and £250,000 are divided by the number of associated companies plus one. The limits are also proportionately reduced where the accounting period is less than 12 months. The rate of corporation tax affects the post-tax profits available to extract as a dividend, and also the impact of the corporation tax deduction for payments of salary or bonuses, and the associated employer's National Insurance.

If no profits are extracted there will be no income tax to pay and no National Insurance, but the company will pay corporation tax at the relevant rate on the profits. Retaining profits may be attractive if the funds are not needed outside the company, particularly if the shareholders have utilised their personal allowances elsewhere.

Accumulation may also be attractive if the shareholder has significant other income and any profits would be taxed at the higher or the additional rate.

However, if the shareholder has no other income, it is likely profits will need to be extracted to cover living expenses. Extraction will also prevent the personal allowance being wasted and allow utilisation of the basic rate band. Taking some dividends will also prevent the dividend allowance from being wasted. See Tips 70 and 71 for the optimal salary depending on whether the EA is available.

Profits extracted as a salary or bonus are deductible for corporation tax purposes, as is any associated employer's NIC. Profits extracted in the form of pension payments (see Tip 85) are also deductible for corporation tax purposes.

As noted in Tip 74, once an optimal salary has been paid, it may be beneficial to extract further profits as dividends.

For 2023/24, the first £1,000 of taxable dividend income is taxed at a zero rate. To the extent that the personal allowance has not been fully utilised, dividends can also be extracted free of tax to use up any remaining personal allowance. So, if a salary has been paid equal to the secondary threshold for 2023/24 of £9,100, it is possible to pay dividends of £4,740 (using the remaining personal allowance of £3,470 and the dividend allowance of £1,000) before any income tax is payable.

Beyond this level it may be preferable to leave funds in the company if they are not needed outside as the extraction of any additional profits will trigger an income tax charge.

Extraction Or Accumulation?

Reginald is the sole director and shareholder of his one-man company.

In 2023/24, he has other income of £200,000. Although his company has made profits, Reginald is an additional rate taxpayer and does not wish to pay further tax at the additional rate (45%) or the additional dividend rate (39.35%). As he has no other dividend income, he pays a dividend of £1,000 to utilise his dividend allowance for 2023/24 and receives the £1,000 of dividend income tax-free.

To avoid paying high tax rates, he retains the remaining profits within the company. His intention is to extract them in the future when he is able to do so at a lower marginal rate.

77. Impact Of Corporation Tax Rate On Distributable Profits

From 1 April 2023 (the financial year 2023), the rate at which a company pays corporation tax depends on the level of its taxable profits. As dividends can only be paid from retained profits, the rate at which a company pays corporation tax will affect the level of its post-tax profits, and consequently the amount of dividends a company can pay. Where the company is paying tax at a higher rate from 1 April 2023, it may be necessary to review the dividend policy as the company may no longer have the retained profits available to pay dividends at the same level as previously.

Where a company has no associated companies, the corporation tax rate is 19% if profits do not exceed £50,000 and 25% where profits exceed £250,000. Between £50,000 and £250,000, corporation tax is charged at a rate of 25% less marginal relief.

Marginal relief is found by applying the formula:

$3/200 \times (U - A) \times N/A$

Where:

U is the upper profits limit (£250,000 where a company has no associates).

A is the company's augmented profits.

N is the company's total taxable profits.

Augmented profits are taxable profits plus dividends from group companies. If the company is a standalone company and has no group dividends, A is equal to N and the formula can be simplified to $3/200 \times (U - A)$.

The effect of marginal relief is that the company's effective rate of tax increases from 19% to 25% as profits increase from £50,000 to £250,000. However, due to the gradual increase, the marginal rate of tax in the marginal relief zone is 26.5%. If the company has associated companies, the limits of £50,000 and £250,000 are divided by the number of associated companies plus one. The limits are also proportionately reduced where the accounting period is less than 12 months.

If the accounting period spans 1 April 2023, it will need to be split and the profits apportioned to the period to 31 March 2023 and that from 1 April 2023. The tax is calculated on each part according to the rates applying at the time. The limits must be proportionately reduced when working out the corporation tax on the post-1 April 2023 profits.

Impact Of Corporation Tax Rate On Distributable Profits

S Ltd is a family company. After paying salaries it has taxable profits of £300,000. The company has no associated companies. It has a policy of extracting all retained profits as dividends.

For the year to 31 March 2023, corporation tax was payable at the rate of 19% – a corporation tax bill of £57,000, leaving the company with retained profits of £243,000 which it can distribute as dividends.

For the year to 31 March 2024, assuming the taxable profits remain at £300,000, the company will pay corporation tax at 25% – a corporation tax bill of £75,000, leaving the company with retained profits of £225,000 to pay out as dividends.

The company will need to review its dividend policy, as it no longer has sufficient retained profits to pay the same level of dividends as previously.

78. Use An Alphabet Share Structure

Where there are several shareholders, it is possible to minimise the total tax bill on extracted profits by first using each shareholder's personal allowance (if available), dividend allowance and then the remainder of their basic rate band, rather than paying all the dividends to one person who will pay tax on dividends at their dividend marginal rate.

However, unlike salary there is no flexibility to choose how much to pay each shareholder as dividends must be paid in relation to shareholdings. This restriction can be overcome by having different classes of shares for each shareholder so the dividend paid to each shareholder can be tailored each year.

This kind of share structure is often referred to as an 'alphabet' share structure as it is usual to designate different classes of shares by different letters of the alphabet, e.g. A ordinary shares, B ordinary shares, C ordinary shares, etc.

Note: careful consideration should be given to the rights attaching to each class of share where the aim is to preserve future entitlement to business asset disposal relief (previously known as entrepreneurs' relief) (see Tip 98).

Use An Alphabet Share Structure

DEF Ltd is a family company. Nick and his wife Rachel are shareholders and directors. Nick holds 100 A shares and Rachel holds 100 B shares.

In 2023/24, Nick has other income of £14,000 and Rachel has no other income. The personal allowance is set at £12,570 for

2023/24. Nick has used up his personal allowance of £12,570 and £1,430 of his basic rate band.

The company has post-tax profits of £60,000 they wish to extract as dividends.

As a starting point, it is possible to pay dividends of £1,000 to Nick tax-free to utilise his dividend allowance and to pay dividends of £13,570 to Rachel tax-free (to use both her personal allowance of £12,570 and her dividend allowance of £1,000). This leaves £45,430 to pay as dividends. Nick has £35,270 of his basic rate band remaining (£37,700 − £1,430 − £1,000) and Rachel has £36,700 of her basic rate band remaining (£37,700 − £1,000). As long as neither receives a dividend which is more than their remaining basic rate band, the remaining dividends will be taxed at 8.75% (a combined tax bill of £3,975.12 (£45,430 @ 8.75%)).

Had all the profits of £60,000 been paid to Nick as a dividend, the associated tax bill would have been £11,095 ((£1,000 @ 0%) + (£35,270 @ 8.75%) + (£23,730 @ 33.75%)).

By having different classes of shares and paying dividends to both Nick and Rachel, their combined tax bill is reduced by £7,119.88.

79. Timing Of Dividends

The timing of dividend payments can determine the tax payable. If the dividend allowance and basic rate band have already been utilised for one tax year, delaying the dividend until the start of the next tax year can save tax.

Likewise, if the personal allowance and dividend allowance for a year have yet to be fully used, accelerating the payment will allow any unused portion to be mopped up.

Where the business has retained profits, it may be viable to extract them in 2023/24 to use up allowances and lower rate tax bands that may otherwise be wasted.

It should be noted that the dividend allowance falls to £500 from 6 April 2024. Consequently, delaying a dividend beyond April 2024 may increase the tax payable on it if the dividend allowance for 2023/24 remains available.

Timing Of Dividends

Bob is the director and sole shareholder of his one-man company.

He is deciding whether to pay a dividend before the end of the 2023/24 tax year. In that year he has other income of £25,000. He has retained profits in the company of £100,000.

For 2023/24, the personal allowance is £12,570, the dividend allowance is £1,000 and the basic rate band is £37,700.

His other income of £25,000 uses up his personal allowance of £12,570 and £12,430 of his basic rate band, leaving £25,270 of his basic rate band available.

As he has not used his dividend allowance, the first £1,000 of any dividend paid is tax-free. This will use up £1,000 of his remaining basic rate band, leaving £24,270 available. If he needs to withdraw further funds from the company, he will pay tax at 8.75% on the next £24,270 of dividends paid (a total of £2,123.62). Thereafter, the dividend tax rate increases to 33.75% (costing him £337.50 in tax for each additional £1,000 of dividends paid). Once this level is reached, he may prefer to delay taking the money until a later tax year when his marginal rate of tax is lower.

Note: once his income reaches £100,000 his personal allowance will start to abate. It is lost completely for 2023/24 where income exceeds £125,140. For 2023/24, tax is payable at the additional rate where income exceeds £125,140. The dividend additional rate is 39.35% (tax of £393.50 on each additional £1,000 of dividends paid).

80. Anticipated Profits

For a dividend to be paid legally by the company, it must have sufficient retained profits from which to pay the dividend. If the company is loss making and there are no retained profits, the company cannot pay dividends. However, funds can still be extracted by means of a salary or bonus or extracted by other means (such as rent, pension contributions, etc.). Paying a salary or bonus will incur a National Insurance charge on the director if the amount paid exceeds the primary threshold, and a National Insurance charge will fall on the company if earnings exceed the relevant secondary threshold and the associated employer's NICs are not covered by the employment allowance. Where the company anticipates making profits, another option is for the director to take a loan from the company in anticipation of a future dividend, clearing the balance on the loan account by paying a dividend when the company is in profit.

However, a benefit in kind charge may arise in relation to the loan if the amount outstanding exceeds £10,000 at any point during the tax year.

Further, if the loan account is still overdrawn nine months and one day after the end of the accounting period and the company is a close company (broadly one with five or fewer shareholders), section 455 tax is payable on the outstanding balance of the loan, at a rate of 33.75% where the loan was made on or after 6 April 2022.

Anticipated Profits

At 31 March 2023, M Ltd, a family company, has a negative balance sheet. The lack of retained profits means that it is not possible to pay a dividend.

Bill, the director, holds all the ordinary shares in the company. His wife and son hold A class shares.

During the following year, Bill takes out a director's loan of £30,000 to allow him to meet living expenses. The accounts for the year to 31 March 2024 are prepared in May 2024 and show a healthy profit.

The company declares a dividend of £40,000 in respect of the ordinary shares which is credited to Bill's loan account, clearing the overdrawn balance.

A benefit in kind tax charge is payable by the director on the benefit of the loan and the company must pay Class 1A NICs on the amount charged to tax.

By using the director's loan account rather than paying a salary it is possible to save tax and National Insurance, suffering only the benefits in kind charge on the loan and the associated Class 1A NICs.

The director will, however, have to pay tax on the dividend that is declared to clear the loan.

As the loan account balance is cleared before 1 January 2025, the date on which corporation tax for the year to 31 March 2024 is due, there is no section 455 tax for the company to pay.

81. Bonus Or Salary To Meet Living Costs

Although paying a dividend rather than a salary will often be a more effective way of withdrawing profits, if the company is loss making and has no retained profits this will not be possible (but see Tip 80) and it may be necessary to pay a salary or a bonus to enable the director to meet his or her living costs.

Although from a tax perspective, it makes no difference whether a salary or bonus is paid, if the shareholder is not a director, paying a bonus can be the more efficient option as less employee's National Insurance may be due.

However, if the employee is a director, there are no National Insurance savings to be had by paying a bonus rather than a higher salary, as directors have an annual earnings period for National Insurance and their National Insurance liability is recomputed on an annual basis at the end of the year.

Bonus Or Salary To Meet Living Costs

Grace is an employee in the family business but not a director. For 2023/24 she receives a salary each month equal to the primary threshold of £1,048 per month. She is 30.

She wants to know whether it is better to receive additional salary of £2,000 a month or a bonus of £24,000 payable in December 2023

It is assumed that the employment allowance has already been utilised. Employer's National Insurance of £40.02 per month is payable by the company on her salary (13.8% (£1,048 – £758)).

If she takes the additional salary, she will pay additional employee National Insurance of £240 (12% of £2,000) per month (£2,880 a year) and the company will pay additional employer NIC of £276 (13.8% of £2,000) per month (£3,312 a year).

If she is paid a bonus of £24,000 in December 2023 (in addition to the regular monthly salary of £1,048) she will pay employee's NIC on the bonus of £794.10 ((12% x (£4,189 – £1,048) + 2% (25,048 – 4,189)). The company will pay additional employer NIC of £3,312 (£24,000 @ 13.8%).

Paying the bonus will reduce the employee's NIC paid saving Grace £2,085.90 (£2,880 – £794.10).

This is because by paying a lump sum bonus rather than monthly payments of additional salary, much of the bonus is liable for employee's National Insurance at the additional rate of 2%, rather than the main rate of 12%.

The National Insurance paid by the employer is the same regardless of which route is taken.

82. Loss Making Companies

A company can only pay a dividend if there are sufficient retained profits from which to pay the dividend. There are no such restrictions on the payment of a salary.

Salary payments are deductible for corporation tax and there is no restriction on the payments where this creates or augments a loss.

In formulating an extraction policy in this situation, it is also necessary to take into account the way in which the loss is relieved. Carrying a loss back and setting it against profits of the previous year may generate a tax repayment, which may be valuable to the company.

Note: there may be company law considerations to take into account if the company's balance sheet is negative.

Loss Making Companies

During the year to 31 March 2024, the company makes a profit of £10,000 before paying the director/shareholder. The company has a negative balance sheet. As there are no retained profits, it is not possible to pay a dividend as hoped so instead the company pays the director a bonus of £40,000 (on which employer's NICs are £4,264.20 ((£40,000 – £9,100) @ 13.8%). The director has not drawn a salary and it is assumed that the employment allowance has been used up elsewhere.

Taking account of the bonus and the associated employer's National Insurance turns the profit into a loss of £34,264.

If the company had sufficient profits in the preceding 12 months to utilise the loss, carrying the loss back would generate a tax repayment of £6,510 (19% of £34,264).

83. Employing Family Members

In a family company situation, it may be beneficial to employ family members, such as children or spouses/civil partners, in order to extract profits from the company and to utilise unused personal allowances.

Care should be taken to ensure that the family member does some work in return for the income to avoid challenge from HMRC. Also, where the family member is not a director, they will need to be paid at least the National Living Wage (£10.42 per hour from 1 April 2023) if they are aged 23 and over or, if under the age of 23, the National Minimum Wage at the rate appropriate for their age.

The same principle can be extended to utilise basic and higher rate bands to reduce the overall family tax bill.

It should be noted that only directors have an annual earnings period for National Insurance. Where the employee is not a director, their earnings period will correspond to their pay interval.

See Tip 69 on paying a small salary to preserve state pension entitlement and also Tip 78 on having different classes of shares to pay different dividends to different shareholders. This can be beneficial to make use of each family member's tax-free dividend allowance, even if the person has income from other (non-dividend) sources.

Employing Family Members

Brown Ltd is a family company of which Ed Brown is the sole director and shareholder.

Brown Ltd employs Ed's wife, Joanna, and his three adult children Max, Zach and Emily, all of whom are aged 21 and over, paying them each £12,570 to utilise their personal allowance for 2023/24. The salary is paid monthly at the rate of £1,048 per month.

As the salary is equal to the primary threshold, no employee's National Insurance is due.

As the employment allowance is available and will shelter the employer's National Insurance on the four salary payments of £12,570, no employer's National Insurance is due.

Ed is a higher rate taxpayer.

By paying his wife and children £12,570 each, which is received tax-free and NIC-free, rather than making an additional salary or bonus payment of £50,280 to himself, the family is able to save tax of £20,112 (£50,280 @ 40%). This strategy will also save National Insurance.

84. Beware The NLW And NMW Trap

Employees aged 23 and over must be paid at least the National Living Wage (NLW). This is set at £10.42 an hour from 1 April 2023 Employees under the age of 23 must be paid at least the National Minimum Wage (NMW) for their age. From 1 April 2023, this is set at £10.18 an hour for workers aged 21 and 22, £7.49 an hour for workers aged 18 to 20 and at £5.28 an hour for workers under the age of 18 (but above compulsory school leaving age).

Dividends do not count towards the NLW or the NMW.

Potentially, the need to pay the NLW or NMW could be a problem if a shareholder/employee is paid a small salary and a dividend. However, a person can work up to 25 hours a week and receive a salary equal to the personal allowance while being paid at the NLW (based on 48 working weeks a year).

However, the NLW/NMW does not apply to directors who do not have a contract of employment with the company, so appointing family members over the age of 16 as directors will overcome any NLW/NMW issues. Alternatively, family members can work on a part-time basis to ensure they remain within the NLW/NMW.

Beware The NLW And NMW Trap

Lucy is a shareholder and works for the family company. She is 26 and she is not a director. She works 15 hours a week. She must be paid at least £156.30 per week (NLW rate from 1 April 2023 of £10.42 per hour) to comply with NLW legislation.

Her brother Brad also works 15 hours per week. However, he is a director without a contract of employment so the NLW/NMW legislation does not apply to him.

85. Pay Pension Contributions

Paying contributions into a registered pension scheme can be an effective way of extracting profits from a family company.

Employer contributions can be made without limit, although they count towards the annual allowance. To the extent it is unused, the annual allowance can be carried forward up to three years. Contributions made in excess of the annual allowance attract a tax charge.

The annual allowance is set at £60,000 for 2023/24. However, this is reduced by £1 for every £2 by which a person has adjusted net income in excess of £260,000 (income including pension contributions) where the person also has 'threshold income' (post-pension contribution income) of at least £200,000, subject to a maximum reduction of £50,000 (ensuring a minimum annual allowance of £10,000). The minimum annual allowance of £10,000 applies where income exceeds £360,000.

For 2022/23, 2021/22 and 2020/21, the annual allowance was £40,000 and was reduced by £1 for every £2 by which adjusted net income exceeded £240,000 where threshold income exceeded £200,000 until a minimum amount of £4,000 was reached. Unused allowances available for 2020/21, 2021/22 and 2022/23 are calculated according to the rules applying at the time.

Where a person has reached the age of 55 and has flexibly accessed a defined contribution pension plan, to prevent recycling of contributions, a reduced annual allowance (the Money Purchase Annual Allowance (MPAA)) applies, set at £10,000 for 2023/24. The aim of this is to prevent recycling contributions.

The lifetime allowance (set at £1,073,100) was lifted from 6 April 2023. It previously placed a cap on the value of tax relieved pension savings. The removal of the lifetime allowance opens the door for profits to be extracted in the form of pension contributions from April 2023 where the director's pension pot had reached £1,073,100. It should be noted that with the removal of the lifetime allowance, the tax-free lump sum is capped at £268,275 (25% of £1,073,100).

Note: employers must comply with the requirements of auto-enrolment. Directors without an employment contract are exempt from automatic enrolment.

Pay Pension Contributions

Bill and Louise are directors of their family company. They each have a registered pension scheme. Both have adjusted net incomes of £100,000.

In 2023/24 the company makes pension contributions of £20,000 each to their registered pension scheme. The £40,000 paid by the company is deductible for corporation tax purposes.

Paying contributions into a registered pension scheme is a tax-effective way to extract profits from the company.

86. Tax-Free Benefits And Expenses

The tax legislation provides exemptions from tax (and National Insurance) for certain benefits in kind.

Making use of the exemptions offers a further opportunity to extract funds from a family company without triggering a tax or NIC charge.

Popular tax-exempt benefits include mobile phones, childcare and childcare vouchers. Providing the benefit rather than the funds with which to buy the benefit saves tax. The costs are also deductible in computing the company's profits.

Note: the alternative valuation rules limit the ability to use salary sacrifice arrangements to take advantage of tax exemptions, as the associated tax exemptions are lost where provision is made via a salary sacrifice arrangement for all but a handful of benefits. The benefit is taxed by reference to the salary given up where this is higher than the cash equivalent value calculated under the normal rules.

Tax-Free Benefits And Expenses

Ravi and Helen are directors of their family company. Their children, Jack and Palie, also work for the company.

The company takes out a contract for four mobile phones and provides each member of the family with a mobile phone. The bills are paid by the company and are deductible in computing profits.

The family members receive the use of a phone tax-free. They do not need to fund a mobile phone from their post-tax income.

87. Pay Interest On Account Balances

If a director has a credit balance on his or her loan account, opportunities exist for paying interest on the balance.

If the personal savings allowance (£1,000 for basic rate taxpayers or £500 for higher rate taxpayers for 2023/24) is available, no tax will be payable on the interest in the hands of the director. No National Insurance is payable either. This makes it preferable to paying a salary.

To keep HMRC happy, the interest should be at a commercial rate and not excessive.

The interest paid is deductible in computing the company's profits as long as it is actually paid to the director (rather than merely credited to the director's account) within 12 months of the end of the accounting period. The company should deduct tax at the basic rate of 20% from the interest and pay it over to HMRC on a quarterly basis.

In the current climate of rising interest rates, this option for extracting profits in the form of interest should be explore.

Pay Interest On Account Balances

Derek has lent money to his family company to fund expansion and his director's account has a credit balance of £50,000. He is a higher rate taxpayer.

The company pays interest at a rate of 5% per annum. The interest received by Derek of £2,500 must be included on his self-assessment return. £500 of it is covered by the personal savings allowance. It is paid to him net of basic rate tax of 20%, but he can reclaim the tax deducted on the interest covered by his personal savings allowance from HMRC.

The company enjoys a corporation tax deduction for the interest paid. It must return details of the tax deducted to HMRC on form CT61 on a quarterly basis and pay the tax deducted over to HMRC.

88. Making Loans To Directors

Funds can be made available to a director by making a loan from the company to the director. Although there are tax consequences of making loans, it is possible for the director to have the use of the money for up to 21 months free or for a minimal cost. The rules also apply where a director's current account is overdrawn.

Under the close company rules for loans to participators, a tax charge arises on the outstanding loan balance if the loan has not been repaid nine months and one day after the year end (the normal corporation tax due date). The rate of tax is equal to the upper rate of dividend tax. This is known as a 'section 455' charge. It is charged at the rate of 33.75% where the loan was made on or after 6 April 2022.

An income tax charge will also arise under the benefit in kind legislation if the director has loans outstanding at any point in the tax year with a balance of £10,000 or more if the loan is interest-free or if the interest paid on the loan is less than that payable at the official rate (set at 2.25% from 6 April 2023). If the loan is repaid by the corporation tax due date, there is no section 455 tax to pay. The benefit in kind charge, should one arise, will be cheaper than paying interest on a commercial loan. In this way, a loan from the company can be a cheap source of funds.

It should be noted that anti-avoidance provisions apply to prevent the loan being repaid to avoid the tax charge and the funds subsequently being reborrowed within a 30-day period or where there is an intention to reborrow the funds at the time the repayment is made (even if this is outside the 30-day period). However, the anti-avoidance provisions do not apply to repayments and reborrowing of less than £5,000, providing limited planning opportunities to reduce the tax payable.

Making Loans To Directors

Ivan is a director of a family company. The company prepares accounts to 30 November.

On 1 December 2021 Ivan borrowed £40,000 from the company. This is at the start of the accounting period to 30 November 2022

The loan is repaid on 25 August 2023, which is within nine months of the accounting period end in which the loan was made. Consequently, there is no tax to pay on the loan balance.

However, Ivan must pay a benefit in kind charge on the loan. This spans three tax years.

The loan is outstanding for 126 days in 2021/22 and the official rate of interest is 2%. The cash equivalent of the benefit is £276 (£40,000 x 2% x 126/365).

Assuming that Ivan is a higher rate taxpayer, he will pay tax on the benefit of the loan of £110.40 The company will pay Class 1A NIC of £38.08

The loan is outstanding for all of 2022/23. The official rate of interest is 2% and the cash equivalent of the benefit is £800 (£40,000 @ 2%), costing Ivan £320 in tax and the company £116.24 in Class 1A NIC (£800 @ 14.53%).

In 2023/24, the loan is outstanding for 142 days. The official rate of interest is 2.25% and the cash equivalent of the benefit is £350 (£40,000 @ 2.25% x 142/365).

The associated tax payable by Ivan is £140 and the Class 1A NIC payable by the company is £48.30 (£350 @ 13.8%).

Ivan has the use of £40,000 for almost 21 months for a total cost of £772.62 (tax of £570 and Class 1A NIC of £202.62).

This is equivalent to an interest rate of 1.1% – considerably less than if he had taken out a commercial loan.

89. Small Loans To Directors

As illustrated in Tip 88, making a loan to a director can be advantageous.

Under the benefit in kind rules, no tax charge arises in respect of an employment-related loan if the balance outstanding on the loan does not exceed £10,000 at any point during the tax year.

This means that it is possible for a director to enjoy a tax-free loan of up to £10,000 for up to 21 months free of charge.

90. Loans Written Off

Beware of the special rules that apply where a loan to a participator in a close company is written off. Most family companies are close companies and the rules will bite when writing off an overdrawn balance on a director's loan account. However, where there are no retained profits, writing off a loan can be preferable to making a salary or bonus payment.

For income tax purposes, the amount written off is treated as a distribution (like a dividend). If the dividend allowance is available, the first £1,000 of the dividend is tax-free (being taxed at the zero rate). Thereafter, it is taxed (2023/24 rates) at, respectively, 8.75%, 33.75% and 39.35% to the extent that it falls within the basic, higher and additional rate bands. As the dividend tax rates are less than the rates payable on a payment of a salary, writing off a loan where it is not possible to pay a dividend will trigger a lower tax bill than making an equivalent bonus payment to clear the loan.

However, unlike a dividend, NIC is payable on a loan written off. For 2023/24, this will cost the director 12% or 2% depending on whether his or her income exceeds the upper earnings limit and will cost the company 13.8%.

From the director's perspective, the tax and National Insurance implications of writing off a loan are a hybrid of the dividend and salary treatments – tax applies as for a dividend and National Insurance applies as for a salary or bonus payment.

However, there is a sting in the tail – no corporation tax deduction is available for the loan written off.

Depending on the tax and NIC position of the director, rather than writing the loan off, it may be preferable to leave it outstanding as, once the NIC charge is taken into account, it may be cheaper to pay the section 455 tax charge on the outstanding loan, particularly as this is recovered if the loan is eventually repaid.

Where the loan is written off in the capacity of a shareholder rather than as an employee, strictly speaking NIC should not be due. However, this is a tricky area and professional advice should be sought.

Loans Written Off

Jenny has a loan of £20,000 from her family company, in which she is director and shareholder. The loan was taken out in 2019. The company is considering writing off the loan.

It is assumed that the National Insurance employment allowance is not available to set against any employer's National Insurance that may arise.

If the loan is written off in 2023/24, she will be treated as receiving a dividend of £20,000. If it is assumed that she has received a salary equal to her personal allowance, but has no other income, the first £1,000 of the dividend is tax-free as it is covered by her dividend allowance.

The remaining £19,000 is taxed at 8.75%, generating a tax bill of £1,662.50 (£19,000 @ 8.75%). She will also pay NIC at 12% on the amount written off (£2,400, being 12% of £20,000). The company will pay NIC of £2,760 (13.8% of £20,000). The tax and NIC cost of the write-off is therefore £6,822.50.

However, if she has a salary of £55,000 and is a higher rate taxpayer, she will still receive the first £1,000 of the dividend tax-free (as it is covered by her dividend allowance), but the remaining

£19,000 is taxed at the dividend higher rate of 33.75%, generating a tax bill £6,412.50.

She will also pay National Insurance of £400 (£20,000 @ 2%) and the company will pay NIC of £2,760 (£20,000 @ 13.8%).

The total tax and NIC cost of the write-off is £9,572.50. If the loan is left outstanding, the company must pay corporation tax of 33.75% on the normal corporation tax due date. This will cost the company £6,750, which is cheaper than the cost of writing off the loan.

If any part of the loan is subsequently repaid, the associated section 455 tax can be recovered.

91. Extract Profits In The Form Of Rent

Where the business is based at home or at another property owned by the director personally, it is possible to extract profits in the form of rent paid for the use of the home office or other premises.

Although the rent is taxable in the hands of the director, there is no National Insurance to pay. Further, the company can deduct the rent in computing its taxable profits for corporation tax purposes.

If the director/shareholder has losses from other property rentals, paying rent will enable those losses to be mopped up. This is because losses from a property rental business can only be offset against profits from that business.

Where rent is paid by a company to a director, it is advisable to draw up a rental agreement between the director and the company.

Note: it is not possible to use the property allowance of £1,000 on rent by a personal or family company to a director of that company.

Extract Profits In The Form Of Rent

David is a director and shareholder in his family company, which is run from his home. The company pays him rent of £400 per month for the use of the home office.

David also has two properties which he rents out. In the tax year in question, he makes a loss on those properties of £5,000.

The rent from the family company is taken into account in computing the profits or losses of the property rental business and the rent of £4,800 received from the company is offset against the loss of £5,000 from the other properties to give a net loss of £200.

As the rent paid to David by the company is offset by other property losses, David pays no tax on it and is able to utilise the property income losses from his other properties.

The company enjoys a corporation tax deduction of £4,800 in respect of the rent paid to David, saving corporation tax.

Chapter 7.
Employing People

92.   Pay PAYE And File Returns On Time
93.   Beware The Salary Sacrifice Trap

92. Pay PAYE And File Returns On Time

Penalties are charged if PAYE is paid late on more than one occasion in the tax year. The penalty is a percentage of the tax paid late. The percentage depends on the number of occasions in the tax year when payment has been made late.

Systems should be put in place to ensure payment reaches HMRC on time. Where payment is made electronically, cleared funds must reach HMRC's account by 22nd of the month. If payment is made by cheque, the cheque should reach HMRC by 19th of the month. Where the due date falls on a non-banking day (Saturday, Sunday or bank holiday), payment should reach HMRC by the last banking day before the due date.

Late payment penalties are charged in-year on a quarterly basis.

Interest is also charged on payments made late. It is charged in-year after the outstanding amount has been paid.

Under real time information (RTI) employers are required to provide details of pay and deductions to HMRC electronically (via a full payment submission (FPS)) on or before the time at which payment is made to the employee. Where no payments are made in the tax month, HMRC must be advised of this by means of an employer payment summary (EPS).

Penalties apply to RTI reports filed late. A penalty will be charged where an FPS is not received as expected and HMRC have not received an EPS to indicate that no FPS was due. No penalty is charged for the first month in which returns are made late. Thereafter a fixed monthly penalty applies, which depends on the number of employees in the PAYE scheme. The penalties will be levied in-year on a quarterly basis.

HMRC allow a three-day period of grace before a penalty is charged. However, this is a concession not a three-day extension to the filing period and it should not be relied on. HMRC may penalise employers who routinely file within this three-day window.

93. Beware The Salary Sacrifice Trap

The opportunity to use salary sacrifice arrangements to take advantage of tax exemptions is now limited. The alternative valuation rules apply to most benefits when they are made available under an optional remuneration arrangement (OpRA), such as a salary sacrifice or flexible benefits arrangement, or one where a cash alternative to the benefit is offered instead.

Under the alternative valuation rules, the benefit is valued for tax purposes at the higher of the salary foregone or the cash alternative offered and the amount computed under the normal cash equivalent rules. Where the rules apply, the benefit of any associated tax exemption is lost.

However, salary sacrifice arrangements remain beneficial for those benefits to which the alternative valuation rules do not apply. These are:

- employer-provided pension savings;

- employer-provided pension advice;

- childcare vouchers;

- employer-supported childcare;

- workplace nurseries;

- employer-provided cycles and cyclists' safety equipment (including 'cycle to work' schemes); and

- low emission cars with CO_2 emissions of 75g/km or less.

Instead, the benefit is valued using the normal cash equivalent rules (which for exempt benefits is zero). For low emission cars, the benefit is valued using the company car rules.

Under a salary sacrifice arrangement, the employee gives up cash salary which is liable to tax and employee and employer NIC in return for an exempt benefit. The employee saves tax and NIC and the employer saves employer NIC. By swapping cash salary for an exempt benefit to which the alternative valuation rules do not apply, it is possible to save tax and employer and employee NIC.

Beware The Salary Sacrifice Trap

Jake employs several people in his business. He operates a salary sacrifice scheme to allow employees to take advantage of tax exemptions.

Katie joined her employer's childcare voucher scheme prior to 4 October 2018. She takes advantage of the salary sacrifice scheme. She is a basic rate taxpayer and swaps £2,860 of cash salary for childcare vouchers of £55 per week. The vouchers are exempt from tax and NIC.

In 2023/24 she saves tax of £572 and NIC of £343.20, so is £915.20 a year better off. The company saves employer NIC of £394.68. Everyone wins.

However, if Katie had swapped £600 for an employer-provided mobile phone, under the alternative valuation rules, the benefit of the mobile phone would be valued at £600 (the foregone salary). The benefit of the associated exemption would be lost. Katie would be taxed on a benefit worth £600 and her employer would also pay Class 1A NIC.

Salary sacrifice arrangements are only beneficial for a handful of exempt benefits.

Chapter 8.
Using Losses

94. Loss Relief Options For The Self-Employed

95. Carry Back A Trading Loss For Corporation Tax Purposes

96. Don't Miss The Deadline To Take Advantage Of The Extended Carry Back Rules

94. Loss Relief Options For The Self-Employed

If you make a loss in your trade, profession or vocation there are various ways in which that loss can be relieved. It is important to consider all the options to ensure that best use is made of the loss. This may be particularly relevant for businesses that suffered losses as a result of rising prices and energy bills.

The general rule is to obtain relief for tax at the highest rate of tax possible (as this will generate the biggest repayment) and as early as possible.

The options are to set the loss against:

- other income for the tax year in which the loss is made;

- capital gains of the same year;

- total income and gains of the previous tax year; or

- future profits of the same trade.

Where the cash basis is used, the loss must be carried forward and utilised against later profits of the same trade. However, the government is consulting on proposals to widen the cash basis, including removing some of the restrictions on loss relief.

Special rules apply to losses in the early years of a trade (see Tip 28) and to losses on cessation (see Tip 101).

For a limited period only, it is possible to carry back trading losses for 2020/21 and 2021/22 and, for corporation tax purposes, losses for accounting periods ending between 1 April 2020 and 31 March 2022 for three years rather than the usual one year (see Tip 96).

As it is not possible to tailor how much of the loss is used, if the loss exceeds income for the year of the claim, your personal allowance will be lost. For individuals, seeking to preserve personal allowances should form part of the loss relieving strategy.

Loss relief must be claimed. It should also be noted that certain income tax reliefs, including loss reliefs, are capped at the greater of £50,000 and 25% of income. This may impact on the optimal loss relieving strategy.

Loss Relief Options For The Self-Employed

Elliot is self-employed and has been in business for many years. In the year to 31 March 2024 (tax year 2023/24) he makes a loss of £20,000. He prepares accounts using the accruals basis.

He has other income of £15,000 in 2023/24 and capital gains of £5,000.

In 2022/23 he had income of £40,000.

The best course of action is for him to set the loss against his income of 2022/23 as this will generate a tax repayment of £4,000 (£20,000 @ 20%).

If he sets the loss against other income of 2023/24, he will lose the benefit of his personal allowance. Similarly, there is no point extending the claim to capital gains as these are covered by his annual exemption (set at £6,000 for 2023/24).

The best result is obtained by carrying the loss back.

95. Carry Back A Trading Loss For Corporation Tax Purposes

As with individuals (see Tip 94) companies should take care to use any losses that they make effectively.

Where a company makes a trading loss, the loss can normally be relieved by carrying it back and setting it against the profits of the preceding 12 months as long as the company was carrying on the same trade in accounting periods that fall in the preceding 12 months. If the previous period was profitable, carrying the loss back will generally be the preferred option as it will generate a corporation tax repayment. For companies struggling with cash flow difficulties, this can provide a welcome cash injection.

For a limited period only, it is possible to carry the loss back three years rather than the usual one. The extended carry back applies to losses for accounting periods ending on or after 1 April 2020 and on or before 31 March 2022 (see Tip 96).

If the loss cannot be utilised by carrying it back, it can be carried forward and set against future trading profits.

Special rules apply to terminal losses (see Tip 101).

If the company is a member of a group, the loss can be surrendered to other group companies.

Carry Back A Trading Loss For Corporation Tax Purposes

As a result of high energy prices, UVW Ltd makes a trading loss of £20,000 in the year to 31 March 2024. In the year to 31 March 2023, it made a trading profit of £35,000.

The company makes a claim to carry back the loss to the year ended 31 March 2023.

This generates a corporation tax repayment of £3,800 (£20,000 @ 19%) (plus interest).

96. Don't Miss The Deadline To Take Advantage Of The Extended Carry Back Rules

To help businesses that have suffered losses as a result of the Covid-19 pandemic, for a limited period losses can be carried back for three years, rather than the usual one. This can be very helpful in generating a much-needed tax repayment. The extended carry back is available for individuals/unincorporated businesses and companies. However, there is now only a limited window in which to take advantage of this.

For individuals, the extended carry back was available for losses of 2020/21 and 2021/22. For an established business, a loss for 2020/21 is one for an accounting period that ends between 6 April 2020 and 5April 2021. Likewise, a loss for 2021/22 is a loss for an accounting period that ends between 6 April 2021 and 5 April 2022. Different basis period rules apply in the opening and closing years of the business.

The extended carry back rules allowed a loss for 2020/21 to be carried back against trading profits from the same trade for 2018/19 and 2017/18 to the extent that the loss is not relieved by setting it against income and gains of 2020/21 and 2019/20. The loss must be set against profits of a later year before those of an earlier year. The deadline for claiming relief under these rules for a 2020/21 loss has now passed.

Likewise, the rules allow a loss for 2021/22 to be carried back against trading profits from the same trade for 2019/20 and 2018/19 to the extent that the loss is not relieved by setting it against income and gains of 2021/22 and 2020/21.

The loss must be set against profits of a later year before those of an earlier year. Where a claim has been made to set a loss for 2020/21 against other income for 2019/20, this takes precedence over a claim under the extended carry back rules. A claim to take advantage of the extended carry back rules for a 2021/22 loss must be made by 31 January 2024. The loss that can be carried back for each year is capped at £2 million. The loss relief cap does not apply to losses carried back under the extended carry back rules. The claim cannot be tailored to preserve personal allowances.

Similar rules apply to companies, allowing losses for accounting periods that end between 1 April 2020 and 31 March 2022 to be carried back against the trading profits of the previous three years, rather than the usual one year. Unlimited trade losses may be carried back one year to the previous accounting period.

The loss that can be carried back under the extended carry back rules for accounting periods ending between 1 April 2020 and 31 March 2021 is capped at £2 million, as are losses for accounting periods ending between 1 April 2021 and 31 March 2022.

The loss must be set against the profits of a later period before those of an earlier period. A claim must be made no later than two years from the end of the accounting period in which the loss was made. For example, a company that made a loss in the year to 31 March 2022 has until 31 March 2024 to make a claim under the extended carry back rules.

If from 1 April 2023 the company is likely to pay corporation tax at a rate in excess of 19%, consideration should be given as to whether it would be better to carry the loss forward – relief would be obtained later but at a higher rate.

Don't Miss The Deadline To Take Advantage Of The Extended Carry Back Rules

RS Ltd prepares accounts to 31 March each year. It makes a loss of £40,000 in the year to 31 March 2022. In the previous year, it made a profit of £20,000; in the year to 31 March 2020, it made a profit of £15,000 and in the year to 31 March 2019 it made a profit of £50,000. It makes a claim to carry back £20,000 of the loss to the year to 31 March 2021 (generating a corporation tax repayment of £3,800), to carry back £15,000 of the loss to the year to 31 March 2020 (generating a corporation tax repayment of £2,850) and to carry back the remaining £5,000 of the loss to the year to 31 March 2019, generating a corporation tax repayment of £950 – a total repayment of £7,600.

The relief must be claimed by 31 March 2024.

Chapter 9.
The End Of The Business

97. Plan Your Exit Strategy

No one can, or will want to, work forever and there will come a time when you want to pass on, sell or wind up your business, hopefully to be able to enjoy the fruits of your labour.

To achieve the best possible outcome, it is advisable to plan your exit strategy at least a couple of years in advance. Some people find it useful to set a planned retirement date and use this as a deadline to work towards. Planning considerations will include:

- whether you wish to retain any ongoing involvement, for example in a consultancy or advisory role;

- whether you need to groom a successor;

- whether you wish to pass on the business to family members;

- whether you wish to withdraw capital from the business and how it will be funded;

- whether you wish to sell any shares;

- how ownership of the business will be shared in the future;

- how transfers of shares or assets can be arranged in a tax-efficient manner;

- if selling the business, whether you are selling shares or assets;

- how the best price can be obtained; and

- how the consideration should be structured.

It is essential that professional advice is obtained well in advance to achieve the best possible result.

98. Claim Business Asset Disposal Relief

Business asset disposal relief (previously known as entrepreneurs' relief) provides relief against capital gains tax on qualifying gains made by an individual on the disposal of all or part of the business, the assets in the business after it has stopped trading and shares in a personal trading company. HMRC Helpsheet 275 has more details on the relief.

Gains that qualify for business asset disposal relief are taxed at 10% up to the maximum lifetime limit. The lifetime limit is set at £1 million for qualifying disposals on or after 11 March 2020. Prior to this date, the lifetime limit was £10 million.

For those with income and gains in excess of the basic rate limit, this relief is very valuable and can save tax of up to £100,000 (£1 million @ 10%).

However, its availability is contingent on certain conditions being met. The conditions must be met throughout the qualifying period.

This is the period ending on the date the asset was sold or business ceased, if earlier. The qualifying period is two years for qualifying disposals that take place on or after 6 April 2019.

Where shares are sold, the qualifying period is the two years ending on the date that the shares are sold, the date that company ceases to be a member of a trading group, or the date on which it stops trading.

The conditions that must be met to access the relief depend on the type of disposal. If you dispose of all or part of your business, you must either own it directly or be a partner in the partnership that owns it.

If you dispose of assets following cessation, you must own the business directly or be a partner in the partnership that owns it. The assets must be disposed of within three years of the date on which the business ceases.

If the disposal is of shares or securities in your personal company, you must hold at least 5% of the ordinary share capital and that holding must give you at least 5% of voting rights in the company.

You must also be entitled to at least 5% of the company's distributable profits and at least 5% of its assets available for distribution to equity holders in a winding-up or meet the alternative test of 5% of the sale proceeds if the company is sold. You must also be an employee or officer of the company or of a company in the same trading group.

The conditions must also be met throughout the qualifying two-year period.

Spouses and civil partners are each entitled to their own lifetime limit of £1 million for business asset disposal relief, potentially doubling the tax savings on offer.

Both spouses or civil partners must meet the qualifying conditions.

The individual must also be an employee or officer of the company or of a company in the same trading group.

Shares can be transferred between spouses and civil partners on a no-gain no-loss basis. Transferring shares two years before the planned disposal date will ensure both parties meet the conditions and maximise relief. Shares can also be transferred to pass the gain from one party to another to maximise relief.

When planning an exit strategy action should be taken to ensure that the qualifying conditions are met throughout the applicable qualifying period. Planning ahead is essential.

Claim Business Asset Disposal Relief

John has operated as a sole trader for many years and wishes to retire. He has planned ahead for the disposal making sure that he has met the conditions necessary to qualify for business asset disposal relief. The business ceases on 31 May 2023 and he disposes of assets used in the business on 28 August 2023, realising a gain of £60,000.

He has other gains in the year which utilise his annual exemption and is a higher rate taxpayer.

He meets the conditions for business asset disposal relief. The gain is taxed at 10% generating a capital gains tax bill of £6,000.

Had he not met the conditions for the relief, he would have had to pay capital gains tax of £12,000 on the gain (£60,000 @ 20%).

Claiming business asset disposal relief saves tax of £6,000 (£60,000 @ 10%).

99. Gift Hold-Over Relief

Business assets may be given to other members of the family. In this situation gift hold-over relief may be claimed. This allows the gain to be 'held over' so that the tax on it is deferred until the recipient sells the asset.

This generates cash flow advantages.

Gift Hold-Over Relief

Nigel has been a sole trader for many years operating in business as a mechanic. He wants to retire and pass the business to his son, so gives him his workshop.

He originally bought the workshop for £20,000 and at the date he gives it to his son it has a market value of £60,000. He makes a gain of £40,000.

The gain is held over. When his son sells the asset, his cost is the market value of £60,000 less the held-over gain of £40,000, i.e., £20,000.

The tax is deferred and there is nothing to pay by Nigel when making the gift of the workshop to his son.

100. Overlap Relief

In the opening years of an unincorporated business some profits may have been taxed twice because of the way the basis period rules worked in the opening years of the business.

The basis period rules are being reformed and from 2024/25 the profits of an unincorporated business will be taxed on a tax year basis. The 2023/24 tax year is a transitional year for businesses that do not prepare accounts to 31 March/5 April. Any overlap profits which have not already been relieved will be relieved in the transitional year.

Overlap Relief

Ian has been in business for many years preparing accounts to 31 October each year. He has overlap profits of £10,000 which have yet to be relieved.

The 2023/24 tax year is the transitional year during which the basis of assessment moves from the current year basis to the tax year basis. Ian is assessed on the profits for the year to 31 October 2023 (the standard part) plus the profits for the period from 1 November 2023 to 5 April 2024 (the transition part) less his overlap profits of £10,000.

The overlap profits are relieved against the transition part of the profits, the net amount being spread over five tax years from 2023/24 to 2027/28 inclusive.

101. Terminal Loss Relief

Special rules apply to terminal losses. This relief may generate valuable tax repayments.

Individuals

A person may decide to stop trading if they are making losses. Special rules apply to relieve terminal losses.

A claim for terminal loss relief can be made if the person permanently ceases to carry on a trade and makes a terminal loss. The terminal loss is the loss made in the period beginning at the start of the final tax year and ending with the date of cessation, plus any loss from the period starting with the date 12 months prior to the date of cessation and ending on 5 April prior to cessation. The terminal loss may be relieved against the profits of the trade for the final tax year and previous three tax years. Relief is given against a later year before an earlier year.

Alternatively, the loss can be set against total income (and extended to capital gains) of the year of the loss and/or the preceding year.

Terminal Loss Relief: Individuals

Barry is self-employed and has been in business for a number of years. He prepares accounts to 31 March each year. His trade ceases on 30 June 2023.

He makes a profit of £10,000 for the year to 31 March 2023 and a loss of £16,000 for the period from 1 April 2023 to 30 June 2023. He has overlap profits of £5,000 to relieve.

His terminal loss is £13,500 ((9/12 x £10,000) – £16,000 – £5,000).

He makes profits of £9,000 for the year to 31 March 2022 (taxed in 2021/22) and £25,000 for the year to 31 March 2021 (taxed in 2020/21).

He claims terminal loss relief.

The profits for 2022/23 have been taken into account in computing the terminal loss.

The loss is set first against 2021/22 (£9,000) with the remaining £4,500 being set against the profits of 2020/21.

Companies

Terminal loss relief is also available for the loss made by a company in its final accounting period. The loss can be carried back and set against profits of the previous three accounting periods. Relief is given against the most recent year first.

The relief must be claimed.

Terminal Loss Relief: Companies

DEF Ltd prepares accounts to 31 August each year. It ceases trading on 31 August 2023 and makes a loss for that year of £75,000.

It made a profit of £30,000 for the year to 31 August 2022, a profit of £35,000 for the year to 31 August 2021 and a profit of £50,000 for the year to 31 August 2020.

Terminal loss relief is claimed. 11

£30,000 of the loss is carried back and set against the profits of the year to 31 August 2022.

£35,000 of the loss is carried back and set against the profits of the year to 31 August 2021.

The remaining £10,000 is carried back and set against the profits for the year to 31 August 2020.

Carrying the loss back generates repayments of corporation tax plus interest.

102. BONUS TIP: Post-Cessation Receipts And Expenses

Income tax is charged on post-cessation receipts arising from a trade, profession or vocation to the extent they are not otherwise charged to tax. A post-cessation receipt is a receipt that a person receives after a trade has been permanently discontinued which arises from the carrying on of the trade before cessation.

In computing the amount that is charged to tax, a deduction is given for losses and expenses or debits that would have been deductible had the trade continued. No deduction is given for amounts arising directly or indirectly from the cessation itself.

Post-Cessation Receipts And Expenses

After the cessation of the trade, John receives a payment of £5,000 in respect of an unpaid invoice arising from the trade which has been written off as a bad debt.

He incurred costs of £500 in recovering the debt.

He is taxed on £4,500, being the amount of the receipt less the cost of recovery.

Ingram Content Group UK Ltd.
Milton Keynes UK
UKHW020344300523
422450UK00009B/82

9 781739 424909